The Haunted Midlands

The Haunted Midlands

ANNE BRADFORD

BREWIN BOOKS

First published by
Brewin Books Ltd, 56 Alcester Road,
Studley, Warwickshire B80 7LG in 2006
www.brewinbooks.com

Reprinted January 2007

ISBN 10: 1 85858 296 2
ISBN 13: 978 1 85858 296 2

A Cataloguing in Publication Record
for this title is available from the British Library.

Typeset in Garamond Book
Printed in Great Britain by
Cromwell Press.

Contents

1. CENTRAL BIRMINGHAM
Haunted by Henry — Union Street, Birmingham 1
Final Devotions — Digbeth 3
Flat Caps and Overalls — Curzon Street, Digbeth 5
Return of the Night Porter — City Centre 5
Tickled Toes — City Centre 6
Hey, Come on out! — Aston 7
Local Radio Ghosts 8
Two Wives and Three Cats 8
Them Bones — The Mailbox, Birmingham 9
Hauntings at Pebble Mill 10
Hullo and Goodbye 12
Out of my body — The Mailbox 12

2. BIRMINGHAM EAST INCLUDING COVENTRY
Bradford Hall — Castle Bromwich 14
Coleshill 16
The Council Office's Ghost 16
The Vanishing Vicar 17
Red as Blood — Alum Rock 18
Hobnailed Boots — Bordesley Green 19
The Griffin — Garretts Green 19
The Smiling Apparition — Small Heath 21
Screams in the Night — Hay Mills 22
Good Samaritans get a shock — Yardley 22
The Donkey Jacket — Hall Green 24
Solihull 24
The Woman at the Window 24
Phantom Tantrums 25
The Ghost on the Loo 26
The Ancient Gardener — Shirley 27
Coventry 28
A Wartime Tragedy 28
Oh Stop It! 29
The Lost Clock 31

3. BIRMINGHAM SOUTH
Unearthly visits — Highgate 33
A Winter's Tale — Sparkbrook 34
A Blast from the Past — Balsall Heath 35
Mother-in-law Pays a Visit — Edgbaston (QE) 36
Selly Oak 38
The Other Sister — Selly Oak Hospital 38
The Phantom Thief 39
The Haunted Loo — Cadbury's Bournville 40
The Silent Pedestrian — Northfield 41
The Siege of Hawkesley House — Kings Norton 42
Rubery 42
The Ghost Comes to Tea 42
The Psychic Brother-in-Law 43

4. BIRMINGHAM WEST
Handsworth 45
Through the Window! 45
Flippin' Heck! 46
Smethwick 46
An Arresting Tale 46
I Know What I Saw! 47
Warley, West Smethwick 48
Oh, Not Again! 48
Come With Me 49
Behold Thy Mother! — Quinton 50

5. BIRMINGHAM NORTH
Bombed Out — Hockley 51
The Dark Rider — Witton Cemetery 52
A Sewing Machine Possessed — Sutton Coldfield 53
The Disappearing Priest — New Oscott 53
Lightning Strikes — Streetly 54

6. THE BLACK COUNTRY
The Malt Shovel — Blackheath 56
Dudley 57
Fogs and Orbs — Dudley Castle 57
The Strange Tale of Melissa 59
The Death Rattle 60

Haunted Hooves — Oldbury 61
The Old Couple — West Bromwich 61
Wednesbury 62
The Old Patrick Bar 62
The Ghost Throws Toilet Rolls 63
The Haunted Cat — Bilston 63
Terrified Motorists — Himley Hall 64
The Old Stag's Head — Penn Common 66
Wolverhampton 68
The Phantom Lorry 68
The Coach Driver's Story 69
The Lord is My Shepherd 70
Spirits of a Different Kind 70
The Rippling Bed 71
Forgotten Slippers 72
His Come-uppance 73
Lost and Found — Walsall 73

7. STAFFORDSHIRE
The Coffin — Enville 75
The Spirit Cat — Brownhills 76
Staffordshire Royal Infirmary 77
A Tribute 77
The Lost Daughter 78
Shugborough Hall 80
Are You Alright Duck? — Barlaston 80

8. WARWICKSHIRE
Fulford Hall — Earlswood 82
The Invisible Motorist — Arrow 84
The Cock and the Treasure — Near Stratford 85
The Blue Vase — Wootton Wawen 87
Phantom Footsteps — Welford-on-Avon 88
Stratford-on-Avon 89
Immortalised 89
The Sleepwalker 90
The Man-hating Ghost 91
Frozen with Fear 93
Who's Been Living in My House? — Tiddington 93
The Resident Ghost — Charlecote Park (National Trust) 94

Who Seeks Sir Guy? — Guy's Cliff 94
Royal Leamington Spa 95
Terror at the Hotel 96
The Guardian Angel 97

9. THE COTSWOLDS
Walking the Cotswold Way 100
Goosepimples — Saintbury Hill, near Chipping Campden 100
The Sampler — Ilmington 101
The Milkman and the Cavalier — Edgehill 103
The Peacock Inn — Middle Tysoe, Near Banbury 104
The Phantom Hitch-hiker — Cheltenham 105

10. HEREFORDSHIRE AND WORCESTERSHIRE
Worcester 106
A Presence for Peace 106
Low Spirits 109
Tipstalled — The Malverns 109
Night Nurse Paralysis — Powick 111
Swords and Guns — Evesham Hospital 112
Out of My Body — Sedgeberrow, Evesham 113
Emma Vernon Rises Again — Hanbury 113
Keeping the Light On — Droitwich 115
The Poltergeist — Redditch 115
Shadows at Foxlydiate 117
Squashing a Ghost — Wychbold 118
Bromsgrove 119
Aunty's Apparition 119
Advice from a Ghost 120
Ghostly Dogs and Other Phantoms — Lickey End, near Bromsgrove 121
Septic Tanks and Floating Bodies — Hartlebury 122
Herefordshire 123
In for the Chop — Bromyard 124
Horror at Little Hereford 124
The Bad-tempered Ghost — Hereford Cathedral 125
Look Back in Anger — Shobdon 128

11. SHROPSHIRE
Still Searching — Boscobel House 129
I'm Keeping an Eye On You! — Telford 130
The Lost Church — Ironbridge 132
The Ouija Board — Craven Arms 133
Ladies of the Night — Ludlow 135

12. CANALS
The Grand Union Canal 137
The Phantom Suicide — Hay Mills 137
Shades of Grey — Hatton Lock 137
The Worcester to Birmingham Canal 138
The White Lady of Wasthill 139

BIBLIOGRAPHY 140

About The Author And Illustrator

Anne Bradford

This is Anne's seventh collection of true ghost stories and she has co-authored another three for the Midlands with Barrie Roberts. She has also written or published five local history books. Anne is a retired teacher of English and commercial subjects. Before settling in Redditch, Worcestershire, she lived in Handsworth, Edgbaston, Hockley, West Hagley, Smethwick, Malvern Link, Acocks Green and Studley (Warwickshire) Her husband is a 'Shropshire Lad', her parents settled near Leominster, her in-laws near Telford and she has relatives across the Black Country, consequently she has a wide knowledge of the Midlands. Anne is married to a retired graphic designer who has written and illustrated two books, *The River Severn* and *The River Avon*.

Zora Payne BA (Hons), Artist/Illustrator

Zora is a professional artist and illustrator. As well as illustrating books, magazines and educational material, she teaches art, paints murals, and runs drawing and craft workshops for adults and children. She also undertakes private commissions. She has a key interest in the story-telling potential of illustration and is well known for her detailed 'this is your life' portraits. Her speciality is fantasy pictures.

Thanks To

Those presenters who allowed me to take part in their radio programmes, especially Ed Doolan, Danny Kelly, Dave Ellis, Malcolm Boyden, Nathan Turvey, Keith Middleton, Dave Bradley etc. This book could not have been compiled without their help.

Barrie Roberts, writer, lecturer and consultant on the paranormal who very kindly copy-read the book and gave helpful advice.

David Taylor, Chairman of Parasearch, a regional paranormal research group founded in 1986 to investigate reports of ghosts, hauntings and poltergeists. His sensible comments, based on the latest scientific research, appear many times. Parasearch are always looking for new members. If you are interested in the serious, scientifically-based investigations of the paranormal then this may be the group for you. For further details send a stamped, self-addressed envelope to David Taylor, Parasearch,15 Brier Mill Road, Halesowen, West Midlands, B63 3HA, or e-mail david.taylor@parasearch.org.uk

George Gregg MSc, MA, CertEd, is the Research Officer of Parasearch who has analysed various experiences (including his own) from a paranormal and psychological point of view, giving food for thought.

* an asterisk denotes not real name.

The grim reaper, a symbol of death. Used in the fortune-telling Tarot cards where it simply means that something is ending, perhaps an unsuitable career, a poor relationship or a spell of bad luck.

1. Central Birmingham

If you had stood in the centre of Birmingham a thousand years ago, you would have found yourself in a deserted waste. There would have been very little to see, perhaps one or two huts with wattle and daub walls and thatched roofs. The soil was merely sand and gravel and the few families living here would have found it almost impossible to grow their crops and feed their animals. There was no road junction with passing travellers and no river to use as highway. Birmingham had nothing to offer and should have faded into obscurity.

There was only one way in which it could develop — through trade and manufacturing. The seeds were planted by the enterprising Peter de Birmingham, who established a Thursday market in 1166. It was the first market charter in the whole of the Birmingham plateau. The Bull Ring was probably the village green, and where Edgbaston Street, High Street, Moor Street and Park Street are now, could have been a few rudimentary one-storey houses with walls of wattle and daub, rectangular in shape and with thatched roofs.

Haunted by Henry – Union Street, Birmingham

No doubt, under the foundations of the large stores in High Street and Union Street are the remains of medieval houses going back as far as the 1100s and 1200s. No-one has seen the ghost in the large Union Street store to guess at his age, which could be placed anywhere within the last 1,000 years! Diane* says:

> We call our 'friend' Henry because the premises used to be the old Henry's store. We hear him, catch glimpses of him out of the corner of the eye and most decidedly feel his presence. There are the classic freezing spots – and I do mean freezing. You walk into a wall of cold and walk out the other side – unless he decides to follow one of us around the stock room (his favourite haunt!). Stock gets shoved off the shelves, silly little things disappear and reappear in annoying places, lifts activate on their own, lights go on and off, sensors get set off and doors fail to lock. Someone shouts 'Hullo' or 'Good morning' on the shop floor at about 6 am (time varies with the clocks altering) and bangs on the walls. He has no preference for day or night. All the usual strange phenomena that COULD be explained away but not quite!
>
> He has set 'walks' and is usually 'seen' as a male wearing one of what used to be the common brown workmen's coats. There are, we believe, more than one 'Henry' but we use the collective name to cover all. One is dressed in black with a high collar and rushes about the place and he makes you feel very uncomfortable – not frightened but very uncomfortable. He creeps up behind you and gives the impression of being very curious about what is going on but also slightly annoyed by us.

'Henry', is dressed in black with a high collar. He rushes about the place and makes you feel very uncomfortable... Stocks fly off the shelves.

I have done a few night shifts for various reasons and know 'he' is there, busy in his own world and whenever I have to effect any fitting changes i.e. moving shelves etc, he really gets annoyed. About August he goes quiet until we start the moves for Christmas.

A lot of this sounds like poltergeist activity. Poltergeist is simply German for 'noisy or disruptive ghost'. As you read through the stories you will see that many of them have the same phenomena. Items are moved or thrown around, there are electrical disturbances including the telephone, video and T.V., together with inexplicable noises such as footsteps or loud bangs. There are problems with the water supply, articles disappear and reappear in strange places or not at all, and the inhabitants report a feeling that 'someone is there' and even see shadowy figures. Poltergeist activity has been known since recorded history and is experienced throughout the civilised world but we still await a scientific explanation.

Final Devotions – Digbeth

Birmingham flourished. In the thirteen and fourteenth centuries, as well as being a vibrant trading centre, it attracted workers in leather, iron and textiles. Birmingham had a greater variety of trades than any other city. By 1656 it was a little timber-framed town of about fifteen streets and had expanded into Digbeth, Deritend and Aston.

To appreciate the next story, you need to be reminded of the ecclesiastical history. In 1529 Henry VIII compelled the clergy to acknowledge him as supreme head of the Church in England, in defiance of the Pope. He died in 1547. In 1553, Mary, his daughter by his first wife, Catherine of Aragon, became queen. She aimed to restore the Roman Catholic faith and a stern persecution of Protestants began in 1555. 'Bloody Mary', as she was known, died in 1558. The next section is told by Maggie, a Stores Supervisor, working in Birmingham. Maggie is a historian and says that baiting bulls and bull fighting was only a small part of the public entertainment provided in the Bullring. It was used for public spectacles including executions!

My family (the Healey's) has had its fair share of strange dealings. I think it must be the Celtic blood!

One of my brothers, after being made redundant and having to find work wherever he could, used to work at a factory called "Thomas Haddon and Stokes" situated in Digbeth and now demolished. All that remains is a blue plaque on the outside dedicated to the memory of The Blessed John Rogers. He had the dubious distinction of being the First Protestant Martyr sent to the stake in 1555 by Bloody Mary and executed in February of that year. The factory was built on the site of the original Bull Ring and execution area.

Anyway, as background information, Jim has never married and at one point thought of entering the Priesthood but like the rest of the family has now become Anglican. I mention this because I think that it has direct bearing on what he encountered one night with a pair of his friends at the factory. I think this occurred about 1973/4, give or take a year either side.

Jim came home at 9:30 after his shift absolutely terrified. A big bloke but generally placid, he was still shaking when he told my mother and myself how he and some colleagues had been down in the basement when they heard a shuffling noise. Jim went ahead, being the one least afraid if it proved to be rats, and walked straight into the sight of a middle-aged man, dressed in a long grey shift, head bowed as he moved slowly, reading from an open book, held before him at chest height.

His lips moved but words were not audible and he did not seem to be aware of Jim or his shaking pals. He was, according to my brother, totally absorbed in his book – most likely a prayer book. Jim, to this very day, firmly believes he saw John Rogers saying his final devotions, the night before he faced the dreadful punishment meted out by Bloody Mary. Jim was a Catholic at the time but no longer practising and under pressure to revert to the Catholic faith. Poor John Rogers was in a similar situation, overseen by priests trying to break him and make him recant. Jim, thinks it was for that reason he was privileged to see him.

At first we thought the dates did not tie up. John Rogers was executed on 5th February and Jim saw him on 18th February, but then my intelligent mother reminded my frightened big brother of the change in the calendar by 10 days in the early 18th century.

I don't know if anyone else ever saw anything again, but I do know that Jim was very wary about going to the basement, even though he knew in his heart that the apparition could do him no real harm, that he had seen a picture from the past and was very, very honoured to have witnessed it. Jimmy is now living in South Africa.

Parasearch is a Midland organisation dedicated to investigating the paranormal. If you would like to become a member the address is in the front of the book. The Chairman, David Taylor, writes in *Haunted Holidays*:

It is a commonly held belief among paranormal investigators that ghosts are some sort of 'recording', somehow preserved in the very fabric of a building. The theory became popular through the support of Oliver Lodge, Professor of Physics and Mathematics at Liverpool University, later the first Principal of Birmingham University and an eminent Victorian paranormal investigator. Lodge suggested that grief and suffering are recorded in some way at the place where they are experienced. There has been much speculation as to how this effect, called the 'Stone Tape' theory (after a 1970s television drama) works, with no-one being able to come up with a completely satisfactory explanation.

We shall be referring to the 'Stone Tape Theory' many times in this book.

Flat Caps and Overalls – Curzon Street, Digbeth

We have Alan Brinkworth to thank for bringing this story to our attention. About fifteen years ago he was working at the Lithograve Printing Company in Curzon Street near Digbeth, built in the 1950s on the site of the Aston Nut and Bolt Company. Lithograve bought the building about 25 years ago. While Alan was working there, the Works Manager, Michael Bird, had an unusual experience. Michael explains:

> Late one Friday afternoon I was just standing there talking to Jim Griffiths, the driver, when this guy comes walking through the print room. He waved to us and went up the stairs. I said, 'Who the hell was that?' He was quite robust, about five feet four inches tall and he was wearing a boiler suit, a flat cap and overalls. He reminded me of that bloke, Fred somebody, who used to knock down factory chimneys on television by burning tyres under them.
>
> Jim went one way, up our reception stairs and I went the other way, up the machine stairs, to cut him off. We met in the middle. All the doors were locked and there was nowhere he could have gone. One man was still working up there and we asked him, 'Has anybody else come in here?' and he said that he had been on his own all afternoon.
>
> Alan reports that when some of the other men were on their own in the factory downstairs they have seen a similar character walk across the end of the building. One of the men ran across to see what the stranger was doing but nobody was there. Another time, a man was working late on a Friday when he heard someone call his name. He decided to make a hasty exit.

Sadly, a telephone call to the factory revealed that the ghost has not made its presence felt over the last few years.

There have been several cases where an apparition has appeared on commercial premises. On several occasions it has been recognised as an ex-employee, usually someone who has retired and is missing his old employment. The workers seem to have picked up a telepathic image of the old employee. This raises an interesting question, the definition of a ghost is 'a person's spirit appearing after his death'. If the apparition is of a living person, can it still be called 'a ghost'? Most researchers use 'apparition' to identify appearances of the living and 'ghost' for appearances of the dead.

Return of the Night Porter – City Centre

Many people think that St. Martin's in the Bullring is Birmingham Cathedral. Not so, it is St. Philip's between Rackhams and Snow Hill Station that has been awarded this honour. It was built in the Baroque style in about 1711 designed by a famous architect, Thomas Archer. It was originally surrounded by equally splendid houses and was the residential area of the wealthy, but the houses have all disappeared. However, a few of them have been replaced by exclusive hotels such as the one in the next story:

> I used to work at a hotel in Birmingham, I won't tell you the name but it's opposite the Cathedral. Lots of strange things happened there. One of the young chaps was asked to go upstairs and get something out of the storeroom. He said to me, 'I'm not going in there again, there's a ghost in there'. At another time a person was doing the rounds and apparently she had gone back to Reception all shaky. They asked her what had happened and she said that she saw smoke coming out of the wall and the smoke gradually assumed the shape of a person. Then the smoke drifted up into the ceiling and into the storerooms above where a ghost had already been seen. A waitress was polishing cutlery when she saw a dark shadow cross the room and disappear into the wall. Another member of staff used to finish before me but she always waited for me before she would leave the building. One night, I said to her, 'Why do you always wait for me?' and she told me that one night she was in the lift talking to the night porter. Afterwards she said to the Receptionist, 'I'm glad I've seen so-and-so, I haven't seen him for a long time and I was getting worried about him, I've just been talking to him in the lift'. The Receptionist said, 'You can't have been, he died a few weeks ago'.

In *Midlands Ghosts and Hauntings*, Barrie Roberts explains that some people believe that 'the matrix survives at least some time after death, carrying within it a sort of outline recording of the complete human. Some believe that it remains where the body dies, others that it stays where the body is buried'.

Tickled Toes – City Centre

In the 1700s people were migrating to the towns and cities in their thousands. By 1750 more workers were employed in industry, trade and commerce than in agriculture. Huge numbers of workers flocked to Birmingham with their families, creating a housing shortage. Airless dwellings were hastily erected without sanitation, heating or a water supply. Water came from a communal outdoor pump and the contents of chamber pots were tipped on to outdoor middens. As the 1800s progressed lavatories were provided, usually shared by a number of families, and water was available in the communal wash-house. Most of these houses have now disappeared in slum clearance, however, a Birmingham back-to-back was restored and opened in July 2004. Victorian houses now have an antique value and many have been upgraded and restored. Phil moved into a Victorian end-terraced house near the centre of the city in the year 2000.

> Until recently I lived here on my own. Frequently, I had something brushing across the bottom of the bed, walking up the side and caressing my toes. It was not an unpleasant experience. Occasionally, I have seen the person responsible. She's female, in her early twenties and in a black Victorian dress. I didn't tell anyone.

A few months ago I decided to take in a lodger and having taken in the lodger, I went away to Paris. When I came back, the lodger said to me, 'This place isn't half strange, sometimes at night a Victorian lady comes in, walks along the side of the bed, touches my toes and then fades away'.

Here is one of those strange cases where the person concerned has never seen a ghost before or since, as far as we know the house has never been subject to any violent event, there has been no poltergeist or other unusual activity yet out of the blue a ghost appears, seen by both occupants of the house! From its clothing, it would appear to be from the past. There are as many theories as to why this should happen as there are ghosts but non have been proved. An interesting suggestion is that some kind of time warp takes place. Are they in our time or are we in their time?

Hey, Come on out! – Aston

The ancient parish of Aston became part of Birmingham in 1911. By 1939 Birmingham had become a great industrial city and its contribution to the war effort was tremendous. It comes as no surprise to learn that it was targeted by the Nazis night after night throughout the war. Perhaps the worst night was that of Ash Wednesday in 1941, when more than 650 high explosive bombs fell on Birmingham and about 170 incendiaries were recorded. The bombs fell across the whole of Birmingham, and in Aston, Small Heath, Stechford and Kings Heath alone 50 or 60 houses were wrecked. The following story was told by Millie during a Keith Middleton Show in 2002.

I live in King Street, Aston. Halfway up my stairs is a freezing area and at certain times I can smell a pipe there. One night, I woke up, my husband was fast asleep and a man was standing right over him. I said, 'Hey, come on, out'. He went out through the door although the door remained closed.

The next morning I told a gentleman who lives at the back of my home here and I described the man. He said, 'He's alright, he would never trouble you'. He told me that there were houses on this site before my house was built but they were bombed during the war. The site was cleared and my house was built. In one of these houses lived a man who looked just like the ghost I had described, and he smoked a pipe. In the end, he committed suicide. Evidently, he has been seen several times, he comes here, but I'm not bothered.

David Taylor, the Chairman of Parasearch, a society investigating the paranormal, remarks:

Historically there has always been some confusion about the burial of suicides. This reflects the fact that legally they were criminals if sane, but not if they were considered mentally disturbed. Until 1823 those found guilty of suicide were given a degrading burial in the road, often at crossroads. Often they were staked. This particularly gruesome practice possibly harks back to the ancient belief that seems to pre-date ghosts – belief in the undead. It was believed that those who died either by suicide or without resolving issues in their lives would return as animated corpses, and therefore they needed to be restrained in the grave to stop them walking again after death. There are many stories of the dead walking again after death in medieval chronicles written by the likes of William of Malmesbury, Walter Map and William of Newburgh.

LOCAL RADIO GHOSTS

Hallowe'en, on 31st October, is traditionally associated with 'ghosties and ghoulies'. The festival probably goes back thousands of years. The Celtic new year began on 1st November, the festival of Samain, therefore 31st October was the last day of the old year. It was a time to prepare for winter. The Celts killed off any extra animals to that they wouldn't have to feed them throughout winter, and animals were mated so that they would give birth in the spring. Huge bonfires, were built, probably on top of burial mounds because they believed that these were the gateway to other worlds, and perhaps they danced round them. The Celts believed that on the eve of Samain, all natural laws were suspended and ghosts and demons roamed freely.

The Romans also held the festival of Pomona on 31st October. Pomona was the Roman goddess of fruit and nuts, that's why a lot of the festivities involve fruit and nuts. We play bob-apple and biting an apple hanging on a string.

When Saint Augustine and the early missionaries arrived in the 590s they knew it would be difficult to get rid of the old pagan festivals so they re-dedicated them to various saints so that they became saints' days. They re-dedicated the festival of Samain to All the Saints in Heaven, so that 1st November. is now All Saints Day. 'Hallow' means holy and 'eve' is the evening before an event so hallowe'en is the Holy Eve.

Two Wives and Three Cats

It was on Hallowe'en 2004 that the popular broadcaster, Ed Doolan, voiced his thoughts on the paranormal:

> I'm like the old lady who, when she was asked if she believed in ghosts, said, 'Of course I don't but I'm still scared of them'. I firmly believe that such a thing exists only because I see things and I think 'That ain't natural'.
>
> I'm sitting in the living room. I had dozed off, as I do in the afternoon sometimes. I hear my wife come home, she opens the door from the garage. She goes through and she says, 'I'm going upstairs to get changed'. The house goes very quiet. I go upstairs and say, 'Where are you?' She's not there. I check the garage and she's not there either. Then the phone rings. She's still at work.

She says she will be leaving for home in 30 minutes. How could that be? I saw her with my own eyes, come in and go up the stairs.

I have two Siamese cats. I saw one of the Siamese at the bottom of the stairs, as it often was. Then I walked into the bedroom and both of the cats were sitting on the bed. I went back out to take a second look but the one at the bottom of the stairs had gone. I saw it very clearly. It looked just like a Siamese cat.

Doris Stokes the famous medium came and stayed at my house overnight. We were talking about spirits and she said, 'There are a couple of spirits in your room'. Suddenly the two Siamese cats sitting in the living room, their heads started to move in conjunction with each other. They looked to the right together, they both looked round the room and they looked to the left together and back to the right together. I said, 'What's up with them?' and she said, 'Oh, they can see them, dear'.

A few years ago we heard that a pub in Feckenham was haunted so I went over with Stuart Roper, a broadcaster who has sadly gone. Next to the pub was a big shed, a workshop, which was mega-haunted. The people who worked there were always seeing things. Stuart was taking the Mickey as he stood by the door. He was saying, 'If you are a ghost, come on, let's see you!' Suddenly from inside the door there was a kick – such a bang and the door shook like mad. Stuart did a four-minute mile. I have never seen anybody move out of a car park so fast in my life. But there was no doubt about the bang and the shaking and nothing was in there.

The Chairman of Parasearch, David Taylor, found the incident with the cats particularly interesting and says:

It is said that animals are sensitive to presences that we cannot see or hear. It is certainly true that animals have more sensitive hearing than we do, so perhaps they are able to sense thing we can't. Research carried out by biologist Dr. Rupert Sheldrake suggests that some animals are aware of things before they happen – a form of animal precognition or telepathy. In several experiments Sheldrake was able to demonstrate that cats and dogs left at home seemed aware when their owners were on a return journey back to them. There are also hundreds of reports of animals who seem to sense a supernatural presence and are unwilling to enter certain buildings.

Them Bones – The Mailbox, Birmingham

After a programme with Danny Kelly, the Security Guard on duty mentioned that he had had a problem with a ghost:

We moved into a new house and on the first evening there my eight-year old daughter woke up crying. My wife went up to her and my daughter said that someone had sat on her bed. No-one was there, but my wife could see an indentation in the bedclothes. This happened again, twice, so on the fourth time, I went up and took my dog. As we approached the bedroom its hackles rose and it wouldn't go into the bedroom. My daughter sat there, crying her eyes out. She even described the man who sat on her bed. She said he had ginger hair and ginger beard and was scruffy looking. She even gave us his name. After a few unsettled nights we decided to change the bedrooms round, so we moved her into the front bedroom and we had the back. The first night there we heard footsteps coming up the stairs and various noises and children's voices. I was a non-believer then so I thought nothing of it.

A few days later I went down the road and happened to speak to the old chap at the end of the road. He asked me what problems I had been having and I told him about my daughter. I gave him the name and the description of the person that my daughter had given to me. He said, 'I know who that is, he used to live in your house'. Then he asked me if I had done anything to the garden. I told him I had put in a patio and a pond. He said, 'When you dug the pond, did you find anything, did you find any bones?' Funnily enough, I had found a couple of bones. He asked what I did with them and I said that I had thrown them on the rubbish heap. He said, 'You must dig your pond up, put the bones back and you won't have any more trouble. They were the bones of his dog. The man hung himself in the back bedroom of your house'.

It seemed very strange to me but I did what the chap said and we have had no more trouble since.

Hauntings at Pebble Mill

Local radio stations have now moved to The Mailbox, near to New Street Station, in Birmingham, but until 2004 they were based at Pebble Mill, in Edgbaston.

A security guard who once worked there says:

Pebble Mill had the reputation of being haunted. They had to have one of the studios exorcised, but the basement was the worst. It was a long, dark corridor with small rooms off, used by the artists as changing rooms. The doors would slowly open and close by themselves. No matter what heating was on, it was always cold down there and the further you walked along the corridor, the colder it became.

Mel from a local radio station in Coventry, who had worked at Pebble Mill, rang the studio to say:

When I was working there I suspected that one of those studios was haunted. I felt and saw – only half saw – somebody there. I was working with Ed Doolan once when all his papers shot across the table. When he had finished talking he turned to us and said, 'Did anybody else see that?' Nobody had. He said, 'My papers moved and there was no draught or anything like that'.

Nicola* started work at Pebble Mill in July 1994 as PA to the Managing Editor of the Multicultural Programmes Department.

He wasn't a particularly nice man and had the most dreadful reputation. Anyway, as I had started on a temporary contract, half-way through the year, my Annual leave entitlement was really poor and when it came to Christmas Eve I had used up all my leave. The whole department, save one or two diehards, had now finished for Christmas but my awful boss made me come into work, despite the fact that there was nothing to do. He himself was in but spent about three minutes in his office – the rest of the time he was swanning round the building chatting to anyone he could find. By 10 am (bear in mind we didn't start work there until 9.30 am!) I was bored brainless so I decided to go and see if the restaurant was open so that I could get a coffee. Thankfully it was, though not bustling as it would normally be at 10 am on a weekday. I picked up a cup, placed it under the coffee spout, pressed the button and waited. Just as I reached in to pick my cup up I felt a really hard shove in the middle of my back. It knocked me off balance so much that I spilt the coffee I'd just picked up and scalded my hand. I shouted and turned round immediately but there was nobody anywhere around except a lady from Contracts Department who was over the opposite side of the restaurant ordering a bacon sandwich. She turned round and said to me 'Talking to yourself?' and I told her what had happened. She just said, really calmly, 'Oh that'll be the Pebble Mill ghost' and off she went.

And here's another experience:

Room G47 is the office which is next door to the Pebble Mill Shop on the ground floor. I worked in here for a couple of years as PA to the Managing Director of Daytime & Lifestyle programmes. Sadly my boss's mother had passed away and she took Compassionate Leave for about a week or so. On the day that she was to return to work I went into the office early to make sure that everything was organised and hopefully easy for her to manage on her first day back. We had a coffee machine in the office as we used to entertain a lot of independent programme-makers. My boss had a preference for a particular kind of coffee which we 'hid' from everybody else because it was more expensive. On her first day back I decided to refill her favourite coffee stand but had to climb up on to a footstool to reach the box which was on top of a large wardrobe-style cupboard. On the top there were a few boxes wedged up to the ceiling and I had to knock them quite hard to get them to move. Some of the boxes came tumbling down and knocked off a load of video tapes which had been lined up on the windowsill. I climbed down from the footstool to pick up the tapes and was crouched down on the floor when I 'felt' the office door open – I felt a kind of a draught, and was completely aware of the fact that somebody had come into the office. I stood up and turned around at the same time and what I saw completely took the wind out of me. Standing right in front of me was a very pretty young girl, about 15-18 years old, I think, with long blond, very curly hair. I could only see her from about the waist up. She was wearing a dark green velvet cape with the hood up. There was a trimming of white lace around the edge of the hood, and her hair was hanging down her front, from under it. She was very pretty and had a demure smile. Within seconds she totally faded away right before my eyes. This completely freaked me and I felt the blood draining from my face, body, arms, right down to my finger tips. For a moment I just froze and then I ran to my desk, phoned my friend who worked on the 7th floor to tell her what had happened and she said that she'd come straight down to see me. I sat down and just tried to get my breath back. Tessa who was the Editor of the 'Anne and Nick' programme then came bursting into the office and she stopped dead when she saw the state I was in and I remember her saying, ironically, 'God, you look like you've seen a ghost'. She was really excited when I told her that I thought I just had!

Parasearch members say that they have heard local rumours suggesting that a workman fell to his death during building work at Pebble Mill. Tragic events are often associated with hauntings, and maybe this may help explain why so many strange things have been reported in the building over the years.

Hullo and Goodbye

After Ed Doolan's Hallowe'en broadcast, one of the journalists, Anna, popped her head round the door to say:

I was back-packing in Australia and I stayed in a youth hostel, sharing a dormitory with 5 or 6 people. The security was very good and the door was locked. To my surprise, I heard a little boy crying and saw him standing at the door. I said to him, 'Who are you?' and he disappeared. I asked round and no-one else had seen the little boy and no boy was staying there. I didn't tell anyone or they would have thought I was barmy. It was all very bizarre.

Out of my body – The Mailbox

Some of the anecdotes in this book originated from a local radio phone-in with Danny Kelly on Halloween 2005 and June 2006. At the end of the 2005 programme, Danny sent the author to interview Arshia who works in the Mailbox. Arshia said:

I was sleeping on my back, facing the ceiling, with my hands together on my chest, when suddenly, in the middle of the night, I woke up and I felt as if something was trying to strangle me, I was suffocating. I began rising up and as I was levitating I was spinning round and round. When I looked down, my bed was empty. I was still in my body.

I told my grandmother and she said that this had happened to me because I was not up-to-date reading the Quran and doing my Namaz, and I was not thinking about God enough. She told me not to sleep as if I was dying but to sleep on my left or right side.

Out-of-body experiences are surprisingly common. In this book are another three, in the Worcestershire section.

In earlier times there was a belief that unearthly experiences were linked to a bad conscience. For example, in 1718, in the centre of Worcester, wherever a young lady by the name of Mary Bentall went, the stones flew around 'like brickbats'. She happened to be accused of stealing a silk apron and was brought before the magistrate. He asked her if she had a bad conscience because these strange things happened. Poor Mary went off to prison. Evidently, this belief still exists in some cultures. Strange to say, ever since then, the centre of Worcester have had problems with falling masonry, two people have been injured and one killed.

2. Birmingham East Including Coventry

Most of the eastern side of Birmingham escaped the industrial revolution. Until late Victorian times it remained chiefly farmland, with villages centred round old churches or stately homes. The industry at Castle Bromwich and Coleshill was surrounded by countryside.

Bradford Hall – Castle Bromwich

Castle Bromwich Hall was built in 1557 and 1558 by Sir Edward Devereux. First of all it was a plain, single storey house but a hundred years later it was bought by a man of national importance, Sir John Bridgeman, whose father was Keeper of the Great Seal of England. The Bridgemans were created Barons Bradford in 1792 and Earls of Bradford in 1815. The house was developed as befitted their status.

The house and gardens have a traditional white lady, in fact there is a sighting of her by a Security Guard in *Strange Meetings*. Local legend tells that the ghost is that of Lady Bradford who came to a violent end - in *Strange Meetings* she was murdered by her husband and in the story below she was hung on the third floor. However, there seems to be no record of a violent death in the official documents and the Bradford's rarely lived at the Hall, it was usually let. If any historian can help us here we would be pleased to hear it.

Although the house is used as offices, the gardens have now been renovated and are well worth a visit. Barry was lucky enough to work in this picturesque situation in the early 1970s:

> Back in the seventies times were hard, I had a new wife to support and an even newer baby. Any extra work that came my way was gratefully received and when my regular employer suggested some weekend work I jumped at it.
>
> The job entailed painting offices at Castle Bromwich Hall or Bradford Hall as it is sometimes known. Each office had to be completed in a weekend, starting on a Friday night and having everything back in its place for 8am Monday morning. All went well with the ground floor and first floor offices. The work was easy, just emulsioning the walls and ceiling and painting a transverse beam in each office block. I got very used to being alone in the big old building and got into an easy rhythm with the work.
>
> Then I started on the third, top, floor. The whole atmosphere of the floor was different and the room that I was working in seemed particularly bleak. This room wasn't anybody's office, it was known as 'the meeting room' but was seldom used. Even with the heating on, the room seemed chilled. I put my feelings down to the drawing-on of winter and the long climb up to the second floor with all my paraphernalia. I cleared such furniture as there was in the

room and spread dust sheets on the floor. After opening and stirring a fresh gallon tine of white emulsion I realised that I had to make yet another journey to my van for a new roller sleeve. When I returned to the room I was greeted with the sight of a sea of white paint. The can, which had been standing in the middle of the floor, was lying on its side, its contents covering most of the dust sheets. Cursing, and not understanding, I set about cleaning up the mess. I was now a good hour behind schedule.

Murphy's law states that if a thing can go wrong it will, and Murphy was much in evidence in that room that weekend. By the Saturday evening my nerves were raw and I quite believed that I wouldn't have the room finished on time. Frantically trying to catch up, I set about painting the transverse beam black. In all the other rooms the beams had taken about half a litre of paint to cover them. This beam was sound with a good surface, I had rubbed it down but I just couldn't get the paint to cover. The more paint that I put on the more it soaked up. The beam had all the absorbent properties of a sponge. After a full three litres I ran out of paint and gave up. I never did finish painting that beam.

I did finish the room on time, just, but to look at it you wouldn't have thought it had been touched. I was loading up my van on the Monday morning when the caretaker ambled over for a chat. He was a typical caretaker who lived on the premises with his wife, he pottered about doing odd jobs and his wife did some cleaning in the offices. His first words were, 'You look rough'.

I told him of the events of the weekend and that I had to work so hard I had had barely any sleep. He smiled the smile of one who knows something. 'They do say', he was savouring his privileged knowledge, 'They do say that that was the room where Lady Bradford hung herself, from that same beam that you had all the trouble with'. I had heard enough!

I recounted the events of the weekend to a friend of mine, John, who was at that time vicar of a neighbouring parish. Reverend EJ Penny was so impressed with my sincerity and unease that he volunteered to say a few words in the room before I started on the adjacent office. The next week my good friend blessed the room and in fact, the whole of that section of the building.

After John left and I was alone again in the old building I felt completely at ease. The whole atmosphere had lifted and there were no more accidents, the work went well as before, but I never did paint the whole of that beam.

This last story was told by Barry Wright, a blacksmith with a wealth of industrial experience behind him. Barry has a wonderful collection of spine-chilling tales. Imagine them told in the late evening by the flickering fire of the forge, with the ironware hanging round, glinting in the firelight.

Until about a hundred years ago, many people believed the blacksmith to have strange powers. He worked with two mysterious and basic tools, iron and fire. Village life depended upon him, he shod the horses and most craftsmen depended on him to supply their tools. There are innumerable folk tales about these ancient craftsmen, Saint Dunstan was a blacksmith while Saint Leonard and Saint Clement are their patron saints. Even today, a local blacksmith tells us 'All blacksmiths are 'fey'. Barry will be telling more tales later in the book.

COLESHILL

The Council Office's Ghost

Named after the river Cole which passes through its northern tip, Coleshill was established between 1220 and 1330. Although predominantly rural, it's near junction 4 of the M6, and the M42 is also nearby. Coleshill suffered badly in the English civil war. In 1642, 1200 Parliamentary troops marched through it, looting and pillaging as they went. The old vicarage below or a house previously on the site probably suffered in the destruction. Whether or not this explains the next apparition is anybody's guess.

In the early 1970s James Hollick left the Police Force and was working at Coleshill for Meriden District Council as Assistant Planning Officer. He describes himself as 'general dogsbody for that department' and continues:

> The building was basically an old vicarage but parts had been built on as offices for the Rural District Council. Edward Heath was prime minister at that time and, for some reason, it was decided to change the names and boundaries of many of the Councils in England. The Meriden District Council then came under North Warwickshire.
>
> I was the only one left in my little department in the Council House, everyone else was moved out, but Severn Trent moved in. The building was now all empty except for my offices on the ground floor with Severn and Trent taking up the rest of the ground floor.
>
> One afternoon, I needed a certain plan. I had to go up to the unoccupied top of the building. As I went up, I put the lights on as it was dark. On the top floor were what I think would have been the servant's quarters in the time of the vicarage. There was a long passage running the whole length of the house, about 40 feet (13 metres), and as I got into this passage it was suddenly very, very cold. I thought, 'That's funny' and I felt the radiators but they were warm. It was a Council building and well-heated throughout. Anyway, I got to this little office place where the plans were, I collected them and stepped back into the long corridor. I happened to look behind me and a girl, aged about thirteen or fourteen was standing there, about 4 feet 6 inches or 5 feet (1.5 metres) in height. On her head was a white mob cap and she was wearing a white dress down to her ankles with an A-line skirt. She was looking along the passageway towards me. She was just standing there and then suddenly she had gone.
>
> Anyway, I walked back down to my own office again. A woman had been working there with me and I told her what had happened. She didn't fancy going

upstairs to have a look immediately but she went eventually. She didn't see the girl but I asked her if it was still very cold and she replied, 'Oh yes, I felt the cold!'

Talking to the locals, they tell me that there's an old wives tale that one of the vicars murdered a servant girl. She wouldn't let him have his wicked way and so he killed her. I don't know if there's any truth in the story.

The last paragraph sounds like information obtained from a 'Penny Dreadful'. In Victorian times, pamphlets with lurid and sensational subject matters were published and sold for a penny. They were the popular comics of the day. Sometimes the author took a famous well-known local name from the past and wove a lurid story around the family. Murders, monsters and vampires were favourite subjects and there was often a chaste young girl who ended up murdered. Contemporary researchers have been known to discover these printed pamphlets and take them at their face value.

The Vanishing Vicar

Although the church of Saint Peter and Saint Paul has been heavily restored by the Victorians, there are still medieval parts, such as the 14th century arcades. It also has an outstandingly good font going back to the twelfth century, and its rich collection of monuments are the pride of Coleshill.

A local school often visits the church and sometimes holds a Christmas Festival there. One lunch time, about 25 years ago, four teachers gathered in the church to plan the festival, and one of them tells us:

I was with three other teachers in our lunch hour and we were working out how the children could play the instruments that we were giving to them for the Christmas festival. We were all gathered inside the little curtain round the organ. One teacher was playing the organ while another held a triangle and so on.

We were half-expecting the vicar, so when a figure wearing black robes appeared in church and came down the aisle we assumed it was the vicar. He was the same height as the vicar, about 5 ft 10 or 11 inches (nearly 180 cm), and in those days it was more common for vicars to wear their robes. Three of us saw him through the gap in the organ curtains and the girl who was playing the organ saw him in the mirror. We watched him come three-quarters of the way up the aisle, we stepped out to greet him and nobody was there. We said, 'Where's he gone?' and 'Oh my God?'

There was no time for him to walk out of the door as the organ was one end of the church and the door was the other. The only possibility was that he was hiding in the pews. I wasn't concerned if it was a ghost, ghosts do you no harm, I was far more scared in case it was a person hiding. We looked in every pew and nobody was there. While we were looking somebody pointed out that we hadn't hear the door opening and the door is very noisy. The dark figure didn't make a sound either and it disappeared so quickly. We just looked at one another and said, 'That's right'. One girl wouldn't come back in the church on her own after that.

As we have said, an apparition need not be that of a deceased person. For example, in *Haunted Holidays*, two sisters in Swansea saw a neighbour going up the entrance steps to her house when she was lying in bed in hospital, wishing she were at home. We have all come across experiences of telepathy. Perhaps people can sometimes pick up a telepathic image. Perhaps the vicar, or a vicar in that area, was thinking about the church and the teachers picked up his thoughts.

Red as Blood – Alum Rock

The Eastern side of Birmingham outside the city centre tended to develop with the coming of the railways. As the population expanded, workers discovered that they could live in a pleasant rural setting and commute easily to the city, while manufacturers learned that goods could be received and despatched from better, cheaper premises without the hassle of congested roads. Alum Rock, Bordesley Green, Garretts Green, Small Heath, Hay Mills, Yardley, and Hall Green are all near to the lines from Birmingham to Coventry, Warwick or Stratford. Most of the houses are therefore fairly modern yet we have plenty of ghost stories from them.

When Val Edwards was eighteen, she was living with her family in Alum Rock. Val is very psychic and will be telling us about her experiences in Redditch later in the book. Judging by the next story, her mother seems to have sometimes been able to predict the future.

I had this boyfriend named Brian, he was a bit of a rogue and my mother didn't like him. One day, he turned up in this large black car. My mother wouldn't let me go out in it. She said, 'I saw you this morning covered in red all over your chest'. Mum and I had a big argument but she felt so strongly about it that she locked me in my bedroom. Anyway, Brian went off in the car.

Three hours later the phone rang. The police said, 'Do you know this young man, Brian? He's in hospital'. He had been driving behind a lorry with a load of girders, one of the girders came loose and went through the windscreen and embedded itself in the passenger seat.

When my mother told me the news I was eating a bacon sandwich and I was so taken aback that I squirted tomato ketchup all down my chest. The red my mother had seen was actually tomato ketchup!

When I went to see my boyfriend in hospital, he said that as the girder came towards him he could see my mom standing in front of the car and that frightened him more than the crash.

A psychic ability seems to run in families, usually, but not always, on the female side. If grandmother has 'the gift' it very often surfaces again in a daughter and/or one or more of her grandchildren.

Hobnailed Boots – Bordesley Green

The Birmingham Small Arms factory (BSA) was built in 1861 and working-class houses mushroomed to serve the workers of this and other factories. Gwen was born in Bordesley Green in 1919 in a haunted house:

My father was born in 1880 and lived with his brother who was two years older, in Little King Street. They both used to tell me this story. Now, if people make things up, when they tell the same story over and over again the story varies slightly but they both told me this story many times and each time their version was exactly the same.

My father and my uncle slept in the same bedroom, one at the end of the house on the first floor. When they were young (about 12 and 16), their parents used to go out for a drink. One night, they were larking about as young teenagers do, when, at about 9 o'clock, they heard their parents come upstairs, go past their bedroom door and go into the front bedroom. They rushed into bed and pretended to be asleep. At 11 o'clock they heard them come back again. My brother said they were so terrified they clung to each other all night long.

It frightened my father so much that he stammered until he was 21, then his wife was able to cure him. After that he became a successful businessman.

I lived in the same house for many years, even after I was married. My brother used to have his bedclothes pulled off regularly by an unseen hand. I only heard noises such as hobnailed boots walking in the roof above me where it's not possible to get a cat in. It was so loud it woke me up. I asked my husband to go up and have a look and he said there was nothing there. I thought it might by mice or something, but my husband said the place was covered with dust that hadn't been disturbed.

Poltergeists are usually quite harmless until they begin to frighten the children. If you wish to quieten things down, you have a number of options. If you are a Roman Catholic you can have a word with your priest. If you belong to another denomination you can go to see your local vicar, who may not be able to do anything himself but should put you in touch with the right authorities. The Spiritualist Church will send along a couple of mediums who usually have excellent results and will often find you an interesting spirit or two. But you should be very careful. Sometimes challenging a poltergeist can increase its efforts and apparent strength.

The Griffin – Garretts Green

Garretts Green is part of Yardley, and by the 1920s and 30s most of the land had been covered in factories and housing. This is another of the blacksmith's (Barry) tales:

The world of the night worker is considerably different to that of his daytime counterpart. The night community is smaller and more tight-knit and people are more hospitable. Visitors to your place of work are rare and consequently, when you do receive a visit you tend to be more generous that you would be in daylight hours.

I worked permanent nights for six years as a mechanic for a large haulage and excavating company in south-east Birmingham. The workshop was vast and could accommodate all manner of trucks and heavy construction plant undergoing major repairs. We would occasionally get a visit from a police patrol looking for a cup of tea, or a lorry driver in need of assistance but our strangest visitor was JC.

JC was, I think, of Anglo-Asian descent. He was olive-skinned with long, flowing blond hair. The strangest thing about the man, though, was his dress. He wore a long flowing white robe and open-toed sandals, even in the dead of winter. The first thing that everyone said, without exception, when they first saw him, was – Jesus Christ. For that was exactly who JC looked like, the old Sunday school prints of Jesus giving the sermon on the mount or feeding the five thousand. I suspect, but can't be certain, that JC was homeless. He was certainly always hungry. The man's great talent was as an artist. He would always have a large sketch pad and a few pencils with him and would earn his supper sketching men at work.

A few days before JC's most memorable visit we had suffered a tragedy in the company. One of the machine drivers had been killed by a bulldozer in the firm's yard. Such a thing is very rare and attracts the attention of the authorities. To ascertain the cause of the accident the machine had been bought into the workshop, put in a quiet corner and roped off. Instructions had been issued in the strongest terms that the machine was not to be touched under any circumstances by anyone other than the inspecting engineer. The whole incident was to kept quiet – not a word to anyone.

JC turned up around one o'clock in the early morning and obtained the foreman's permission to be on the premises and said, 'Hello' to the lads on the shift. We were genuinely pleased to see him as most of us had one of his dramatic portraits and his pictures were invariably stunning in their quality. He managed to capture the drama of working on huge machinery in a vast, dark building. JC settled himself somewhere in a corner and the rest of us carried on working.

At three o'clock we all trooped into the canteen for a well-earned tea break and on this occasion to view JC's latest masterpiece. He opened the sketch pad and showed us several of his normal 'men-at-work' type portraits, each fitter happily identifying himself amidst general ribaldry. JC turned the page again, the room fell silent. Depicted starkly in perfect technical detail was the killer bulldozer, all sixteen tons of the beast. Above it, reared up on scaled legs, was the most hideous griffin-like beast I have ever seen. For what seemed an age no-one spoke then someone, probably the foreman, asked what we were all thinking. 'What is that?'

JC spoke quite calmly and in a matter-of-fact voice. 'the angel of death'. JC knew nothing of the machine's history nor why it was in the workshop!

A griffin was a mythological creature with the head, wings and talons of an eagle and the body of a lion. The griffin is supposed to be a symbol of vigilance, vengeance and wisdom and can be found in many a coat of arms. It is, however, a truly awesome-looking creature and is much more appropriate as an angel of death.

The Smiling Apparition – Small Heath

Again, attracted by the Birmingham Small Arms factory, worker's houses spread along the Coventry Road from Deritend in the middle of the 1800s. Vera got married in 1950 and went to live in one of these houses in Small Heath.

It was a little house, two up and two down. One evening I was in my kitchen, I looked across to the living room and an elderly man was sitting there, by the fire. He turned and looked at me and smiled. To my surprise, I wasn't a bit afraid.

I didn't tell everyone because people think you're barmy if you see a ghost, (my mother used to think I was barmy) but a few weeks later I saw a neighbour whose in-laws used to live in the house, and I told her about this ghost and described it to her. She said that she couldn't make any comment as it was her husband's in-laws who had lived in the house. When I saw her again a few days later, she said that she had told her husband what I had seen and from my description he recognised the ghost as his father. He suffered from poor health and he used to spend all day sitting by the fire.

I was in that house for about three years and I saw him about three times. That's the first time I ever saw a ghost. Ever since then, if I go anywhere and there's something a bit off, I can feel it.

Ghosts are often identified. *Midland Ghosts and Hauntings* tells how, in 1986, one of the staff at Aston Hall, Philip Bettam, saw a lady in a flared green dress with a lace collar sitting in one of the chairs. In 1990 Roy Evans was on duty and saw, through a window, the head and shoulders of a lady dressed in green. The following year Martin Brookes was locking up when he saw the same lady in a dark green dress looking out through a window. Mr. Hipkiss saw her in 1992 as he was buffing the oak panelling. They were shown old drawings and photographs to find the identity of the ghost and selected Mrs. Walker, housekeeper to Sir Thomas Holte in 1645. Similarly, at Harvington Hall, a lady was having a cup of tea in the tearoom before going round the house and she insisted that she seen 'an elderly man in old-fashioned clothes looking out of the restaurant window'. She was assured that the tearoom was empty at the time. She later identified the man from a drawing on the wall as Thomas Kemble, a Catholic priest executed in 1679, known particularly because of his last request to smoke a pipe with his gaolers!

Screams in the Night – Hay Mills

The local manor house, Hay Hall, still exists on the Redfern Road, although by 1966 it had become a factory. A local mill owner, James Horsfall, built a church next door to his factory, the church stretches right across the river Cole!

Mike used to be a night watchman at Webster and Horsfall and spoke on local radio:

> It was built on a children's hospital and sometimes we used to hear screaming in the night. When we went to investigate, nobody would be there.
>
> A colleague of mine was a very down-to-earth type of person. He saw a chap leaning against the wall when the factory was closed and everyone had gone home, he asked him what he was doing there and the chap just floated away. My colleague was so terrified that he locked himself in the Time Office and was still there three hours later. He said that the chap he saw looked so real.

Of all poltergeist activity, perhaps screaming is the worst, and much has been made of it in supernatural tales. The crying and screaming of children is a frequent manifestation and particularly distressing to those who hear it. When the Kingfisher Centre in Redditch was first built, security guards often heard a child crying and notified the police, but no child was ever found. When they were in the balcony, the crying sounded as if it was on the ground floor and when they were down below, the noise came from the balcony.

Good Samaritans get a shock – Yardley

Most of Yardley was built in the 1920s and 30s but at its heart is the ancient church of St. Edburgha. She was the daughter or grand-daughter of Alfred the Great (849-901), who held the Danes at bay. Edburgha was abbess of Pershore and also of Winchester. When she died, she was buried at Winchester and miracles were performed at her tomb. Winchester Abbey grew rich from tourists and visiting sick hoping for a miracle. The abbot of Pershore Abbey asked if he could have part of Edburgha's body for a share of the miracles and Earl Odda of Pershore paid for three of St. Edburgha's bones. Unfortunately, the miracles stopped at Winchester and began happening at Pershore. The Abbot of Winchester asked for the three bones to be returned but Pershore refused. The wrangling went on through the centuries until no-one believed in sacred bones any more, then Winchester gave all Saint Edburgha's bones to Pershore. The clerics of Pershore didn't know what to do with them and, as the chancel at

Yardley was being developed, they buried them there. If you believe in sacred bones performing miracles, Yardley chancel is the place to visit.

Here's another tale from Barry the Blacksmith about a factory in Yardley, not far from St. Edburgha's Church:

> It was November the fifth. The rain was absolutely sheeting down and one or two fireworks were making a brave attempt at lighting the sky. Outside in the street a lone figure dressed in a duffle was standing under our one and only street light.
>
> By nine-o'clock break, we, the night shift, were getting concerned about the figure and its welfare. The foreman, Bob, was elected to investigate. The remaining four of us watched from the canteen window as Bob persuaded the figure to come in out of the rain. We heard our illustrious leader take the mystery person into one of the offices, and heard no more for an hour or so.
>
> The rest of the shift had gone back to their various jobs by the time that Bob emerged and I was the first one that he spoke to. He satisfied my growing curiosity with a very sad tale of human misery. The figure was a sixteen-year-old girl who had run away from home. She was pregnant, in fact about to give birth, and had an unsympathetic step-father of whom she was frightened. She had until now managed to conceal her condition from her family, but the game was up. Bob, a father himself, had done what he could practically, he had given the girl towels and hot tea and 'phoned for an ambulance.
>
> Just as he was finishing his tale the ambulance arrived with blue light flashing. Bob led the ambulance crew to the office. Within seconds the entire shift were looking for the girl, the ambulance men were on their radio and the police were being involved. The girl had disappeared and what is more was never found – well not that night anyway.
>
> Some days later I was on my way in to work in my car when I spotted what I thought to be the girl standing near to the lamp post. I pulled up and wound the window down. 'Hello' I said cheerily, 'Are you all right now?'
>
> The girl turned and smiled at me. At that point I saw that she was about twenty, I would think, certainly not a teenager. Before I could apologise for my mistake she replied, 'I'm fine thanks. I often come here. My mother came here the night she died having me and the men were kind to her'.

A similar story is in *Haunted Holidays.* It was pouring with rain when Bob Bierd was returning from a holiday in Devon, driving along the A38. Just outside Tewkesbury he saw a young lady at a bus stop looking cold, tired and wet. He says, 'This was in the 1970s and people were more trusting in those days' and he gave her a lift home. When he went to leave, to his surprise the exit seemed blocked by a fence and he had to find another way out. Some weeks later, he called back at the cottage. The woman who answered the door said that no young girl lived there but she once had a daughter who had been killed in a traffic accident in 1957 in pouring rain.

The Donkey Jacket – Hall Green

Hall Green is a huge modern development (chiefly 1900-1940) built around the Church of the Ascension, which goes back to 1704. Ray's* story takes place in the summer of 1991:

> One Sunday I was working in Hall Green for a friend of mine who owns a number of garages. Some of them have been converted into work units and he has a small car repair business in one of them which he inherited from his father. The garages are behind the houses and shops and are arranged in a triangle.
>
> When it came to lunch time we sat outside our workshop to eat our sandwiches. The garages had the old-fashioned doors, about seven feet (about 210 cm) high with small windows at the top. I saw this man ferreting around and looking into the garages through these small windows. He looked quite shifty. He worked his way round until he was in the far corner of the triangle. I said to my friend, 'What's that old chap looking for?' but he couldn't see him. We walked over to the corner to look for the old chap but nobody was there. The corner of the triangle is all enclosed and there is no way out.
>
> I described him to my friend. I said that he was elderly man wearing a donkey jacket and on the back of the jacket it had in large letters 'LANG'. My friend's reply was, 'I don't like the sound of that, my old dad wore one like that with the same letters on. It sounds like my old dad to me'.

Ghosts very rarely, if ever, appear in a logical way. Their materialisation seems to be quite random. In the above situation, you would expect the ghost to appear to his son, but it was the son's friend who saw him. For example, in *Haunted Holidays*, there's a case in Great Malvern where a widower was very upset because his wife, who had recently passed away, appeared to his domestic help and not to him.

SOLIHULL

The Woman at the Window

A hundred years ago, Solihull was surrounded by many small but impressive stately homes known as 'Halls', some of them dating back to Elizabethan times. There was Berry Hall, Walford Hall, Herewood Hall, Longden Hall, Malvern Hall, Hillfield Hall, Tudor Grange, Sutton Lodge, and many others. David* worked at one of the few halls still in existence.

> Not far from Junction 5 of the M42 is a large fourteenth century hall and the owner is an acquaintance of mine. In the early 1990s it needed some renovation work, so the architect and the builder arranged to meet one of the ladies who owned the property. The architect was first to arrive and he found the front door locked. He walked around and he happened to look up to see

a woman standing at the front bedroom window directly above the entrance to the house. He knocked the door again, wondering why she didn't answer. Again, he looked up at the window and the figure was still there. Then the lady he was expecting to meet arrived in her car. Thinking someone had broken in, they searched the house but no-one was there, the house had been empty.

On another occasion, a lady who was helping in the renovations saw a carriage pull up in the drive outside.

The owners commissioned a review of the property. I was told that they discovered that a previous owner of the house found out that he was not the father of his wife's little daughter and strangled the little girl in grief and distress. He then shot himself in the front bedroom of the house. I have been in that front bedroom and it gives you an unpleasant feeling as you go into the room. There's an oppressive feel to it, the hair stands up on your neck and you feel cold.

As we have no date, it would take weeks to confirm the murder by research. If any historian comes across this case, please could they notify us. Or does the story come from another Penny Dreadful?

Phantom Tantrums

If you go into Borders book shop in Touchwood Shopping Centre and ask for Eileen, she will tell you this story herself:

Way back, in 1980, I was working for Barnbys in Mill Lane, Solihull, which was part of the Midland Educational set-up. Older residents will remember it, as it was there for many years. Before we went home at night we would stack the toys on the one wall upstairs and on the counter and the table, but when we came in next morning one of the toys would be over the other side of the store. It would look as if it had been thrown there, sometimes it was smashed and broken. It happened on and off but only on the floor upstairs. We never found out what it was. Our manageress was attuned to the psychic and she claimed it was a poltergeist.

We were so intrigued that we had a look at the old maps to see what had been on the site beforehand. Solihull was just a village until the 1950s, and on the site where Barnby's stood had been the village school and playground. I think Barnby's was the first store on that site after it had been developed. Across the road were some old worker's cottages that had been knocked down in the 1950s and 60s and Beatties had been built there, on the corner of Warwick Road.

I left Barnby's in 1988. The shop itself closed in 1990 and was taken over by Country in Town, a very nice shop selling furniture and furnishings. They closed about 18 months ago. I went in there to buy some cushions and I was chatting to the girls when I happened to say, 'I worked here about eight years ago'. During the course of conversation one of them asked, 'Did you ever have any problems here? We have found sometimes that if we leave something on the one side upstairs it's right over the other side of the store the next morning'.

That remark was quite independent. Nobody had told her about our poltergeist. It was very odd.

There's a question for which no-one has an answer. If you move into a house which has the reputation of being haunted, do you continue to have problems? In our experience, the answer is probably no, and we think it is very unusual for the activity to continue as it does here.

The Ghost on the Loo

In 90% of ghost stories you can think of a possible explanation. Was the anomaly caused by a reflection, a draft, banging in the pipes, squirrels overhead, or a state where a person thinks they are awake but are actually asleep and dreaming? However, there are those few ghost stories in which you know the person concerned and for which there is no possible explanation. Mark's* story is one of these:

I'm a plumber by trade and one day in 1991 I was working at a house in Solihull by the Land Rover company, fitting a shower for an elderly lady. I parked my van outside, got my bits and pieces and the lady took me upstairs into her bathroom. I said to her, 'I think we should have the shower this end of the bath near the hand-basin so that you can put it over the sink when you want to wash your hair'. She thought that was a good idea.

I hauled everything into the house and I was in the middle of taking the old shower apart when I realised I needed some more tools from the van. When I came back this old chap had perched himself on the toilet, not actually using it but just sitting there. He said to me, 'So that's where you're sticking it'. I explained I thought it was the best place. We had this weird conversation, it sounded as if he wasn't going to be there for long. He said things like, 'As long as she's going to be OK' and 'She's happy with it then'. I finished the work and came out of the bathroom. The lady was waiting for me at the top of the stairs. I said that I'd finished and added 'I can leave you to it now'. She asked one or two questions and I told her, 'Your husband's clarified it with me'. She said, 'What did you say?' I repeated, 'Your husband said that you know where you want it'. She asked who I was referring to, so I described him. I told her everything he was wearing, down to his fob watch, his pin-striped suit with a waistcoat and his collarless shirt, unbuttoned at the neck.

She said, 'That's my husband but he's been dead for some years'. She took me into a bedroom and showed me her husband's suit hanging in the wardrobe which was the one I'd seen, and opened a drawer to show me his fob watch and chain. I felt a cold shiver go up my spine. By this time, her eyes were full of tears. She said, 'At least I know that he's still looking after me'.

I was just leaving when the hairdresser arrived and she told her about it. Her hairdresser remarked, 'You have always moaned about the inconvenience of washing your hair and now he knows you are happy'.

He appeared to me just as if he was an ordinary person. I never thought anything about it at the time.

Here's an interesting comment from David Taylor, Chairman of Parasearch:

In all good ghost stories, ghosts glide across the ground and walk through walls. In fact, in the vast majority of true ghost stories, the ghost or apparition appears physically real, so real in fact, that they are thought to be an actual person at the time. There are many reports of ghosts that have been seen, that have touched people, that have made sounds when they walked, etcetera. So who knows, you may have seen a ghost today and not been aware of it!

The Ancient Gardener – Shirley

Allotments were popularised in Great Britain by the passing of the Allotment Act of 1887. When World War I had been in progress for about two years the shortage of food encouraged the allotment movement. Local authorities were given the power to devote sections of public parks to allotments. Before World War I there were 32,000 registered allotment holders, by the end of the war there were approximately one million. Jenny has an allotment in Shirley:

I was down at the allotment earlier this year (in the summer). The plot next to mine is worked by a young lady. I had a feeling that somebody was there so I turned round, expecting it to be my friend – but there was this man!

He was a young man in old-fashioned wartime clothes. He was wearing those old trousers with a bib and brace, where the straps cross over at the back and fasten on to the bib at the front with two buttons. He was clean shaven with short hair and he was bending down, working with a trowel. I only saw him for a split second but I think his trousers were grey. He looked real, I thought at first he was a proper person. I jumped and he went.

These allotments must have been worked during the war. There are men here in their mid-eighties and they have had allotments here for at least forty or fifty years.

David Taylor remarks:

Ghosts in historical dress are a staple diet of all good ghost reports. What is truly interesting about such reports though, is what they tell us about the phenomena itself. Although we associate ghosts with being dressed in clothes from a bygone era, it is only from about 1680 onwards that ghosts appear in costume from the past. Ghost reports prior to this period are of apparitions dressed in the clothes of the day. This paradox is an interesting one, and still under study.

COVENTRY

In 1086 Coventry was a small rural settlement, but three centuries later, the population had grown to about 7,000 and it had become one of the leading cities in the kingdom. No-one knows precisely why. In medieval times it became the centre of the cloth industry, later noted for its ribbons, watches and sewing machines and in the twentieth century it was well-known for its motor cycles, aeroplanes and cars.

The town grew up around a Benedictine monastery, founded in 1043 by Leofric, Earl of Mercia, which became the fourth richest monastery in England. According to an old legend, Leofric set high taxes on Coventry folk, consequently, his wife, Lady Godiva, begged for their removal, which he promised to grant if she rode naked through the town. This she agreed to do, and the people of Coventry shuttered their windows and remained indoors, except for a tailor who peeped through a chink and was struck blind. Ever since he has been known as Peeping Tom.

In 1940 Coventry was heavily bombed. The old Cathedral of St. Michaels, dating from 1373, was destroyed although miraculously, its 296 feet high spire survived. Its destruction has become a symbol of Britain's war-time suffering, with the new Cathedral rising from the ruins of the old.

A Wartime Tragedy

Mrs. Marriott was in the centre of Coventry on the night of the bombing and related this experience to us in about 1995:

> On the night of the November blitz my young man and I were sitting in the Scala in the centre of Coventry when an air-raid warning came up. A notice was flashed on the cinema screen saying that an air raid siren had been sounded in case anyone wanted to leave the cinema. About an hour later another notice was flashed up, saying that there was intense enemy activity over the city and the film would be discontinued.
>
> For a short while, we just sat there and took no notice. We had sat through these things before and they had just blown over, but then I remembered that my boyfriend was the youngest of three sons and I thought his mother would be worried about him. So I said to him, 'We'd better see if we can get home'. We went out of the cinema and it was obvious that we wouldn't be able to get anywhere. The whole city was on fire and there was glass everywhere which had been blown out of the shop windows. It was terrible, so we went back into the cinema. He said to me, 'Please change seats', so I sat in the aisle seat.
>
> The first bomb landed on the stage and I saw a flash but there must have been another bomb that fell on the balcony. The strange thing is that I distinctly remember that I felt someone put a blanket round me and lift my hands up off

my lap and put them over my face. Afterwards, my face was unscratched but my hands were a mess. I definitely feel I had a protective something.

My young man, aged 19, was killed when the balcony collapsed. When I came to, somebody was saying, 'Please help me with this young man, he's been hurt'. We took him and laid him in the foyer and waited for the ambulance to arrive. Not many other people had been hurt because most people had left the cinema. Another young girl, Gladys, had lost a hand.

We were taken to the Gulsen Road hospital at about five or six in the morning. Nobody told me he had died. The nurse told me to go home and come back later taking someone with me. I had to walk from the hospital to my boyfriend's house. There were no buses, nothing. There was nowhere for them to go. You couldn't tell where you were because all the landmarks had gone. Tram lines had been ripped up and were pointing skywards. Everywhere had been barricaded off. It took me hours to get through. I told his mother that he had been hurt and all that she said was, 'You had better take a clean hanky', so she gave me a clean hanky. She didn't go back with me.

When I went back to the hospital, the nurse told me that he had died. She said, 'We're very sorry, there was nothing we could do for him'. I had to find my way to Tower Hill where his father worked, he was manager of the Co-op. I didn't have to tell him, he knew by the look on my face. We made our way back to his house to tell his mother. You know the phase, 'tearing your hair out'. This is exactly what she did.

The funeral was devastating, It was a communal funeral. A young boy of 16 sat in the road, being violently sick. We were told that he had lost all his family. My father said, 'We have lost our flower, but he has lost his flock'.

I often think about my boyfriend. He would have been 76 on 1st. October.

Why did her boyfriend change seats? It would not have been to improve his view because the film was not being shown. It would not have been to stretch his legs as he moved away from the aisle seat. 'Please change seats' is a curiously brief request. Did he have some kind of premonition that he could save his girlfriend? She, herself, had a surreal experience. Some people might say that she had a Guardian Angel, but if so, why did her boyfriend not have one?

Oh Stop It!

Brian from Coventry told the following story on Ed Doolan's show, one bank holiday Monday:

When I first left school at about 14, I really thought I was being wound up by the two directors of a particular company in Spon Street. The first director kept saying 'Oh stop it Bill, stop it!', and he was getting quite agitated. He was claiming that the second Director kept stroking the back of his head. However, I could see the hands of the second Director and he was busy writing. Then I

Something almost pushed me – there seemed to be a presence… I was almost transfixed, looking at this huge tank... there it was, hidden at the back.

was in the same building on my own around Christmas time and the mistletoe was moving of its own accord. One of the staff claimed to have been pushed down the stairs.

Here comes the cruncher – I was in the building with somebody else and we heard a shivering noise and we thought, because of the way in which the building was put together, somebody was breaking into the building via the attics. These being old buildings, the hatch giving access is in the gable end. We called the police and the police dog wouldn't go into the building.

Subsequently, one of the gentlemen who I was with at that time has carried out some research and he has discovered that, during World War II, a bomb fell on Spon Street and someone was killed. Several people have now claimed that they have seen the apparition of that person.

This sounds like typical poltergeist activity. Sometimes it seems to be accompanied by dark moving shapes of people and very occasionally, a human being is seen. We have three cases where, after various unusual happenings in the house, a man comes into the bedroom and is clearly seen and felt getting into bed with the occupier of the house.

The Lost Clock

Sandra told this story on local radio. There are many tales of clocks stopping when the owner passes away, in fact there is one in the Wolverhampton section, but this is a clock story with a difference.

My father died on 13th September this year. We had moved him from his life-long home to a bungalow only 16 weeks before he died. He had a rather superior clock presented to him for long service when he was 62, from Garrards, the Queen's jewellers. When he was taken into hospital I said to my husband, 'We must bring that clock back to us. It's a family possession and it's the sort of thing that will walk from an empty house and I don't want it to disappear'. My husband went down to the bungalow with our eldest daughter and he couldn't find the clock. I said, 'It's got to be there. He has got his name engraved on it. I don't think he would have done anything with it'.

A little later I went down to have a look. It was getting dark by the time I reached the bungalow. I looked everywhere and I couldn't find it. I stood there and I said out loud, 'Dad, what have you done with it, now you have really put me in it'. Something almost pushed me – there seemed to be a presence – I went through the first door then I was propelled to this other door, that of the airing cupboard. I found that I could hardly move, I was almost transfixed, looking at this huge tank with the red and white jacket. The airing cupboard wasn't big enough to walk into but again I felt as though I was almost pushed and I found I could just squeeze in at the side of the cupboard. And there it was, hidden right at the back. He probably hid the clock just before he went into hospital.

One of the best clock stories was in *Worcestershire Ghosts and Hauntings*, now out of print. Rod Healey, a clockmaker in Catshill, collected a damaged grandfather clock for repair, but while it was in the shop the owner died. Rod was working until two o'clock in the morning, and through an open doorway saw a dark shape standing by the clock. Thinking it was a burglar, he grabbed a milk bottle. When he went closer he saw that it was an elderly gentleman, almost certainly the clock owner, standing by the clock. Another strange thing was that Rod couldn't get the clock to go until this supernatural visit, but afterwards Rod swung the pendulum and it has been going ever since!

3. Birmingham South

Travelling south, one of the surprises is how exclusive residential areas exist side by side with working class areas. For example, Edgbaston, with its large detached Victorian houses, had the back-to-backs of Ladywood to the north and Sparkbrook and Highgate to the east.

Unearthly visits – Highgate

Our journey southward is introduced by Dave Hart:

This story was told to me by my mother many times. Her mother and father were living somewhere in the Highgate area of Birmingham when they heard of a bigger house in Adelaide Street that was lying empty. Gran contacted the council about it, the council moved in and cleared the house out, but at the time my Gran was not told of the house's history.

My mother was born in May 1916, so I think this story would relate to around 1920s. When they first moved into the house my mom and her sister used to complain to their parents that something was pulling the bedclothes off them at night and tossing the girls out of bed. Certain objects would fly across the room. However, gran and grandad would not believe them and it was not until strange things started happening at midnight that anyone listened to them.

Mom said that at midnight as the clock struck 12, the front door would burst open and they would hear this unseen entity enter the house, roam around the table in the living room, then go into the scullery and turn the tap full on, go up the stairs, roam around the first floor bedroom, then up to the top bedroom and the attic. At one o'clock in the morning the spirit would be felt coming down the stairs into the back yard and leave. The same thing happened night after night.

The police dogs would not enter the property at any cost. The local priest was called in on two occasions but had no effect. Eventually the family were rehoused not a hundred yards away in Darwin St, again in a back-to-back house. The story is told that the first night in their new property the same thing happened again, the front door burst open and this spirit was in the house until one in the morning. The second night, my grandad said, 'I have had enough of this', he rolled up the Evening Mail and lit it from the fire, and as the door opened he threw the paper out the door. My mother said that the colours that appeared were unimaginable. After that they never had another problem.

Apparently the police report said that the House in Adelaide Street was the site of a double murder and a suicide. The man of the house was having an affair with his sister in-law, so he killed his wife, he then panicked and killed his sister-in-law, he then went downstairs, washed his hands under the tap, locked the door, went upstairs and hung himself in the attic. The house was in a yard next door to the Carpenters Arms public house, which is still there today and still serves a good pint. When these houses were knocked down the land was cleared and was not built on for many years.

This is the first time we have come across a ghost being laid to rest by the *Evening Mail*. The two girls sound as if they were victims of poltergeist activity with bedclothes being whipped off the bed and articles flying across the bedroom. It has been noted that it does seem associated with young teenagers and usually females and especially when ill or under stress.

Apparently, the 'spirit' moved with them when they moved house. If the history of the house was the reason for the disturbances, why did the 'spirit' move with them?

With regard to the double murder and suicide, the dates are too vague for research, but if any historian should come across an account of this double murder we should be most grateful for a copy.

A Winter's Tale – Sparkbrook

Another lovely anecdote from a back-to-back, this time from Sparkbrook. Most of the houses here date from the second half of the 1800s. It was told at the Worcestershire Skills Show in the autumn of 2001.

> My parents lived in Larcher Street, Sparkbrook. There were no indoor toilets, you had to go down the yard, round the corner and they were next to the wash-house. My mother used to call it, 'The Lav'. One evening, there had been a deep fall of snow and because it was dark, she asked my father to stand on the doorstep and watch her safely to and from 'The Lav'. He stood there, shivering with cold. In the end he got fed up and went indoors.
>
> From 'the lav' you could see out into the street where there was an old gas lamp. As she came out she saw a cowled figure gliding under the lamp. She watched it as it went right along and came up the entry. She fetched her husband they looked round but it was virgin snow and there were no footprints, only hers.

It's amazing what you can learn from footprints, and they feature in many a detective story. The rebuilding of prehistoric animals has sometimes been centred round their footprints, and virtually all the information about the Yeti has come from a few footprints in the snow. We have many examples on record of mysterious prints. *Ghosts, Murders and Scandals (of Worcestershire)* tells of an old church on the Wells Road in Malvern, now known as Body Works. During the first World War a Zeppelin passed overhead and when the vicar's wife looked down there were footprints in the snow going toward the house but none going away. They were thought to be those of the ghost of the Zeppelin pilot. Again, when the Kingfisher Centre in Redditch was first built in the 1970s, security guards who walked across an open section from one car park to another in the rain would look back to find their wet footprints accompanied by another set.

A Blast from the Past – Balsall Heath

If you go into the Book Department of WH Smith in Birmingham and ask for Maggie, she will tell you this story herself. Again, it relates to a back-to-back but this is a back-to-back with a difference.

Here's a little story of an old 'Two-up, two-down' that I lived in as a youngster. It was in Tindall Street, Balsall Heath, and at the back of an entry – but looking at the old Ordnance Survey map of the area it may have been adapted from some sort of farming property as it had the feel of once being part of something 'grander'. It was a strange set of housing as the premises next to ours was huge and boasted tennis courts (long fallen into disuse by the 1960s) and crumbling glasshouses. Genteel poverty: the remnants of a faded era, no doubt. I always got the impression that my house (and the one joined to it) which stood alone at the back of others, at the end of an alley that boasted an old hand water pump, formed part of a far older set of buildings. The door opened outwards and seemed more like a back door than a front one. I think that one had been bricked up at the back of the house but we had no access to there. The range was a huge black-leaded affair with a bread oven integrated on the side and 'arms' that swing out for pots to hang over and other smaller cooking ovens around it, far too big for a house that size. The house was L-shaped with a door entrance in the corner where the short part of the L joined the large living room.

The stairs to the upper rooms twisted sharply from the far corner of the room up to a tiny landing. If one was foolish enough to stand on that landing for any length of time, 'some-one' gripped your ankles and literally tossed you head over heels down the stairs. I remember it all too well. It was a flight of about 14 steps with a sharp twist at the foot and I first recall being tossed head over heels at the age of 4/5 (1962/3) but we all copped it in turn and my mother – a very tiny lady of 4 feet 8 inches came a cropper several times if she was not alert enough.

Just ahead was the smaller bedroom and directly to the right, the big bedroom. In the big bedroom, a lady was often seen sitting on the end of the bed putting on her shoes. She gave me the impression of wearing a blouse with leg-of-mutton sleeves and a black skirt – probably Edwardian A tall man in a tall hat, with thick black beard stood on the landing staring into the small room – but only my brother, Tony, saw him. The man may have been earlier as his hat was more 'Dickensian' – tall coppertank/moleskin with the short coat and breeches of the mid 1850s. Tony was very frightened as he said the man was staring at him. My brother was a tough kid.

If a bed was placed by the one wall the occupant woke up suffering from terrible nightmares – and to this day my sister cannot sleep close to a wall – and she's a tough cookie!

By the big sash window was the old gas mantle and there I saw something like a mist trying to take shape – my sister saw this too. It was like a swirling mass that never quite took shape – or maybe it did but my head was under the sheets by then! Imagine the white 'snow' you see on a T.V. screen when the signal has gone down and that is what it looked like. I saw it only once that I can recall but my sister Noreen – a VERY perceptive lady – saw it several times and said that as it had not hurt her the first time, she chose to ignore it on other occasions – but a vicar friend of mine did suggest that unformed masses such as that were often potentially evil.

Going back to Tindal Street, I have managed to search the 1881 and 1901 census reports and tracked an Elizabeth Sanders living at the address, then known as Laburnum Place. Apparently it was originally attached to farm buildings at the back (market gardens and dairies thrived in Balsall health in the 19th century). It seems Elizabeth was brought in from the country to care for elderly relatives. She never wed nor had kids and I get the impression she did not like children in the house. However, the lady who sat on the end of the bed may not have been Elizabeth as I had the impression from her clothes that she was Edwardian.

I recall being frightened a lot of the time and always looking over my shoulder without really knowing why. We left the house in 1967 as part of the slum clearance programme of the inner cities/bombed buildings left still from the war and it has since been demolished – ostensibly to allow room for the nearby school to expand, but oddly enough the land has never been built upon.

Time permitting, I intend to look closer into that hidden history of Balsall Health because folk have the impression of the area as being an inner city slum area. Court houses DID sit side by side with large, impressive middle-class houses.

I do have a map of the area from the mid 1880s my partner copied for me from the library and one can see just how rural it had been until the 1870s/80s.

Several people have said that when they see a ghost, it starts off as hundreds of silver or white dots. A housemaid who saw an apparition in the garden of the Clock House (now demolished) at Fockbury, near Bromsgrove, remarked, 'The Star Trek crew materialising looked much the same'.

Mother-in-law Pays a Visit – Edgbaston (QE)

Although Edgbaston is within walking distance of the city centre, in Pevsner's book, 'The Buildings of England - Warwickshire', he describes Edgbaston as 'a smart and fashionable appendage to Birmingham'. The Lord of the Manor of Edgbaston would not allow any commercial ventures or cheap housing. Birmingham University and the Queen Elizabeth Hospital are both in that area.

The latter was started in 1933 and, together with the Medical School, was Birmingham's major project between World Wars I and II.

The next narrator has two special relatives; a niece, Deborah, now in her thirties, and Deborah's husband, George, who is 41.

> George is a hundred percent health fanatic, he only eats foods that are good for you and exercises every day.
>
> Fifteen months ago he had a major heart attack and was rushed into the Queen Elizabeth hospital. The doctor said he had to have a triple heart bypass there and then. Deborah and her daughter were allowed to sleep in the family room.
>
> It was touch and go and four days after the operation there was no change in his condition. The nurses went to fetch Deborah and her daughter and as they went back to the ward they caught a brief glimpse of someone walking away from George's bed but they thought it was a nurse and didn't think twice about it.
>
> They sat by George's bed and he was awake. He was white and shaking. They said, 'Are you alright?' George said he had a bad fright and continued, 'Debbie, I have just been speaking to your nan (who had died). She said, 'Get off that fat backside of yours and get better, Deborah needs you to look after her. Because you are so fit and healthy you are going to survive'. Then she walked round the bed and held my hand'. We thought he was hallucinating and said, 'George, you have to go back to sleep'. We sat there, talking and a nurse came in. She said to George, 'What were you doing with that grey-haired lady? You know you are not supposed to have visitors without my permission. Next time, please let me know'. When they showed some surprise, the nurse told them that she had looked in earlier and seen an elderly lady with glasses sitting there, holding George's hand. He said, 'It was my mother-in-law. She has been dead for four years'.
>
> When the doctor came he said, 'Because you are so fit and healthy you are going to survive'. Exactly the same words as the mother-in-law. We often talk about it. Before this happened if you mentioned ghosts or spirits he would laugh. Now he is 100% believer.

We have lost count of the number of times we have heard the phrase, 'I didn't believe in ghosts until I saw one!'

George Gregg, Msc, MA, CertEd is the Research Officer of Parasearch. He has put forward a series of explanations for the above from various points of view. Have a look through them and see, in your opinion, which explanation is most likely:

Explanations from a paranormal point of view:

1. This may have been a spectral visitation from the dead mother-in-law, as George described. She may have been looking down from the after-life and seen him dying or giving up, and decided to give him a prod.

2. He was dreaming, or thinking about his mother-in-law. She had died recently and he may have thought his turn was on the way.
3. The nurse may have picked up the grey-haired lady by Extra Sensory Perception. George may have picked up the doctor's words by precognition (whilst dreaming) and embroiled them into a vision of the mother in law.

Psychological Explanations:

1. It is quite common for those close to death to see visions of their dead friends and relatives and this may be something to do with changes in the brain's biochemistry. There have been cases in the past - rare, but not unheard of, where people have auditory hallucinations announcing illness or recovery.
2. George appears to have been a health fanatic and has probably read extensively about health, illness and signs and symptoms. Therefore an aspect of his unconscious mind could have been trying to communicate this to him.
3. If he was cared for in Intensive Care, then he may well have suffered from social and sensory deprivation, a common experience in hospitals, especially if he was prescribed painkillers or tranquillisers - perfect recipe for hallucinations. Often we are subconsciously aware of illness and this can become embroiled in our dreams and visions.
4. A visitor or a patient may have wandered in from another department. Often, the Elderly Mentally ill with dementia get lost and mistake other patients for their relatives. Or he had a genuine visitor that he assumed was his mother-in-law due to similarities of appearance. Naturally from this perspective the doctor's words were simply a coincidence.

SELLY OAK

The railway reached Selly Oak in 1876, joining the Worcester and Birmingham canal. This led to a rapid suburban development. The roads tend to be lined with rows of Victorian terraced houses, very popular with students of Birmingham University, nearby.

The Other Sister – Selly Oak Hospital

David Buckley's story has been on our files for some years but not included in books for lack of space. This time we were determined to give it an airing:

> In 1968 I was Night Superintendent at Selly Oak Hospital. In those days we had two children's wards out in the grounds, they were both single units, one was for babies and the other for children over five. The wards were out in the

grounds on their own and at night you had to find them in the dark, and very dark it was, too.

There was always talk about an old sister who would be hovering around when a baby was very sick. In addition, the girls who worked regularly on that ward swore that there was somebody watching them. As a mere man and a psychiatric nurse to boot I told them they were barmy.

Normally on each ward during the night there would be one senior nurse and one helper, but occasionally there would be a staff shortage – someone would be ill or something. If the ward was short-staffed, the night sister there would go over and check every half-hour or so. In addition, an experienced night sister would be doing the whole of the rounds.

On this particular night there was only one nurse on duty and she was not the normal nurse. In addition, they had a sick baby who needed intravenous drugs to be topped up regularly. The night sister was very busy and at about 1.30 or 2 am she had not managed to have a break, so I said to her, 'You go and have a cup of tea and I will check everything with that sick baby'. I took a walk over to the baby unit. It was a filthy night, raining cats and dogs. When I got there, the nurse said, 'Oh, the other sister has done it'. I asked, 'Which other sister?' Apparently, the other sister had called in about ten minutes previously and the nurse described her as elderly, with a grey dress and wearing a bonnet with bows under the chin. Well, there was an occasional one or two who still wore a hat with a bow under the chin in the 1960s but they were a very rare breed and certainly none were about that night.

The baby had been checked out and the drugs brought up-to-date. Everything was fine, but to this day I don't know who the hell it was. In those days, you didn't have to sign a register for drugs except for the dangerous drugs so we had no signature. It was very odd.

I know without doubt that that happened. I wrote a statement about it in one of the hospital books and it's still there, buried somewhere in the archives.

At that time I was very down-to-earth and sceptical. It made me think.

There's a happy ending, the baby recovered and soon went home.

The Phantom Thief

The following story was told by Tony from Stechford, on a programme with Dave Ellis who was standing in for Ed Doolan

Me and my mate used to work at Birmingham Batteries at Selly Oak, just off the Bristol Road there, on maintenance at nights. The place was absolutely full of spirits. We had one spirit that used to follow us around, pinching tools. I can't tell you how many nuts we lost. We would put them down and the next minutes they would be gone. One night, I put a spanner down, I went round the other side of a machine, came back and the spanner had gone. There was nobody there, we were on our own on a platform in the middle of the night. It never turned up.

The most common activity of a poltergeist is to hide articles, which has caused many a dispute, especially in a large family. Mostly it seems to be silly little things, like lipsticks, hairbrushes, pens, and so on but occasionally, someone is amazed at the size of something that goes missing. One young lady's jeans kept disappearing. As she says, 'Big things, jeans, where on earth would those go to?' At Trotter Hall near Droitwich, now with its old name of 'The Copcut Elm' the poltergeist spirited away a huge catering-sized metal colander. The staff remarked, 'Where could that possibly go?'

The Haunted Loo – Cadbury's Bournville

Cadbury's was founded in 1824 with a little tea and coffee shop in Bull Street, Birmingham. By 1879 it had expanded sufficiently to be able to build 'A factory in a garden'. At a time when dark, satanic mills were filling the town centres, the Cadbury's factory was set amid green lawns and trees. Houses for employees were spacious and set in wide, tree-lined roads. Because the family were Quakers there were no public houses on the Cadbury estates.

This is the second female supervisor to tell us, in confidence, of Cadbury's ghosts. In *Midland Spirits and Spectres* a supervisor tells how she was instructed to have a word with a young lady who was spreading a rumour about a ghost. However, about two years later, the supervisor followed a lady in black into the ladies' toilets only to find that she herself was the only occupant! More recently, another supervisor says:

> Cadbury's has several ghosts. A little boy has been seen and heard crying several times at the bottom of C block, I have spoken to a couple of engineers who heard him crying and saw him standing in the corner of the room. Evidently, that was where the nut room was situated. A lot of nuts are used in chocolates and they used to be crushed in massive big presses. The workers would put the nuts in the press, close the press, open it and sweep away the pieces. Boys were employed to run in and clean the presses before the next load of nuts went in. It is said that one little boy wasn't quick enough and he was crushed to death in the press. That part has now been demolished.
>
> There was a ghostly smell as well. As supervisor, I would sit on a platform above the women and sometimes, just in the one corner, I would smell this lemon verbena.
>
> The haunted loo was in the top of A block. In those days, you had to go up a flight of steps, to reach it. One of the employees, aged about fifty plus, went up the steps and into the loos. We heard an almighty scream and she came tearing down the stairs. We thought she had fallen over or something but she had seen a person hanging in the toilet. She was so frightened that you couldn't dispute it.

The Silent Pedestrian – Northfield

What a pity that the ghost was wearing a nylon mac, as Northfield's Church, the ancient St. Laurence, has some of the best Early English work in the county, at least 800 years old, and if she had worn an older costume it would have been a wonderful opportunity to investigate the history of the church and make some suggestions as to who she might have been.

Beryl J Percival very wisely wrote down her father's story while he was still alive and the following is taken from her original account:

> My father, Edward or Ted Mason, as he was known, was a very sensible and straightforward man. He served in France during the First World War, survived the horrors with his cheerful and practical way of living and was absolutely reliable and truthful.
>
> His ghost story happened during the 1940s, probably about 1943-4, at Northfield, Birmingham, close to the Worcestershire border. Dad used to work at Cadbury's chocolate factory and walked each morning from our house near Northfield station, along Woodlands Road to catch a bus on the Bunbury Road. I believe the time of this happening would have been about 6.30 am on a summer morning. There was a light morning mist, but no fog. He saw a woman walking towards him, dressed, he thought, in a pale-coloured nylon mac, this was quite shiny, he said, as nylon was, in those days. She passed him by, and he immediately turned round, because it struck him that there was no sound of her footsteps in the early morning quiet, and he wondered whether she was walking barefoot. To his astonishment no-one was there. The pavement on his side of the road at that point was edged by a fence and hedge, with no gap, and there was not time for her to have crossed the road and disappeared into a house. However, he was so amazed by her disappearance that he walked a short way back just to make sure that she had not somehow raced forward fast enough to reach the footpath leading off Woodlands Road to St. Laurence's churchyard. No-one was to be seen, and it was quite impossible for the phantom lady to have turned the corner out of sight along this track in the time. My father said he had no option but to believe that he had seen a ghost.
>
> I think that it was fairly soon after this dad had a serious illness (burst duodenal ulcer – nothing affecting his mind!) but he survived after a close brush with death. I have wondered since whether this experience might have been connected in some way, perhaps a warning. Anyway, he survived and lived to be 80, dying in 1974.

It is said the people who are ill or under stress are more susceptible to the paranormal. Was he picking up a telepathic image?

There's a tradition that female ghosts are tragic heroines visiting the scene of their disastrous lives and although it makes a good story, ghosts who have been recognised tend to be quite ordinary, happy people, like a verger or a housekeeper or a gardener.

The Siege of Hawkesley House – Kings Norton

The Civil War of 1642-1646 was basically a battle of power between Charles I and Parliament. England was brought to its knees. Both armies were often ill-disciplined, unpaid and ill-fed which resulted in rape and pillage throughout the country. Birmingham suffered terribly, for example in April 1644 Prince Rupert and Prince Maurice (Rupert's brother) stole as many sheep and cattle as they could from Birmingham.

Probably, at that time, they were staying in Hawkesley farmhouse, home of the Royalist Middlemore family. Records suggest that it had been converted into a garrison. About this time, the Parliamentarians arrived under Colonel Fox (known as Tinker Fox - his father was a tinker), drove out the Middlemore family and strengthened the garrison. In January 1645, 400 Cavaliers arrived from Dudley Castle to besiege the farm. The next day Charles I arrived with more soldiers. The parliamentarians surrendered and the house was pillaged and gutted. The farm was rebuilt in 1654 but later demolished and Edgbaston golf club now stands on the site.

To see remnants of these ancient battles is very rare and very exciting. When Kevin* was a lad he lived in Kings Norton by Hawkesley Farm.

> One night we were up the fields, playing and mucking around when these misty figures of men with large hats came walking across the field. They had their long sticks with them, I suppose they were pikes. It terrified me. The locals used to say that the roundheads walked across the fields there, but the soldiers I saw were more like Cavaliers.

This is another story from local radio and unfortunately, we were not able to get hold of Kevin's telephone number for more details. If you read this, Kevin, please could you telephone Hunt End Books, 01527 542516?

A famous sighting of an army comes from York Cathedral. A workman was in the crypt when Roman soldiers marched by. He was able to describe them in the minutest detail.

RUBERY

The Ghost Comes to Tea

Rubery is on the south-western outskirts of Birmingham, sandwiched between the Waseley and Lickey Hills and with the huge old Austin Rover concern nearby on the west. In Roman times one of the salt trails from Droitwich went this way. The Joseph Sheldon Hospital closed in the 1990s and the Birmingham

Great Park is now on the site, with its restaurants, cinema, health centre, hotel, supermarket and bowling alley. A nurse from the hospital tells the story:

Teatime was at five o'clock every afternoon, when we fetched the patients from the smaller rooms and took them down to the big room for their tea.

It was getting dark when I started checking the empty rooms to make sure no-one had been left behind. One of them had been occupied by an 80-year old who had died the previous week. I opened the door and looked in and I could swear that she was there, sitting as she usually did in the geriatric chair that tipped back (they don't use them now) in the mauve cardigan that she liked to wear over her dress. I know I uttered a sound of some kind, I gasped or something, then she had gone.

It was a great pity that hospital closed. It was a lovely hospital and we really looked after our patients.

In *Haunted Holidays,* Barrie Roberts explains a theory that every live human being is surrounded by an energy matrix or force field, and 'the matrix survives for at lest some time after death, carrying with it a sort of outline recording of the complete human. Some believe that it remains where the body dies, others that it stays where the body is buried'.

The Psychic Brother-in-Law

In the same town Dorothy* tells us about her unusual brother-in-law. He wants to remain anonymous which is a shame as no doubt the parapsychologists would love to get hold of him for tests.

My brother-in-law is the most unlikely person to have out-of-this-world experiences. He's very brusque and until he retired recently he was foreman in a factory. He's married with two children. These experiences have only been happening to him over the last ten years, it started after my dad died. He's felt dad's presence and he has seen him a couple of times.

My sister and I are living in the house where my dad died. One afternoon, we were struggling to plant a tree in the garden. My brother-in-law was visiting us and he was standing in the kitchen, watching us out of the window. We looked down at the kitchen window and he was crying. We said, 'Whatever is the matter?' He told us, 'Your mum and dad are standing there watching you do that'.

A few weeks after I lost my husband, I had this awful feeling that I just wanted him to hold me. My brother-in-law knocked on the door. He said, 'Your husband wants me to give you a hug'. He wrapped his arms round me and gave me a really big hug.

He told my neighbour something about her mother. He said to her, 'I have seen your mum and she's wearing a beautiful big comb in her hair. My neighbour said to me, 'How did he know that?' When she was young she used to wear her hair long and held it up with a comb. He had only seen her once and then she was old and wore her hair short, and there are no photos of her in the house.

The last episode came when my sister and I were sitting in our front lounge talking to him. Suddenly, all this smoke was swirling round him. I said, 'You're on fire'. He gently moved his hand and it disappeared. My sister thought she saw something forming, she told me that if I hadn't jumped up, something would have happened. It was such a shock. There was no reason why the smoke should be swirling round his head. There was no fire and he wasn't smoking. His only comment was, 'You keep saying you want to see something and now you have'.

He gets very upset when this happens to him. He says, 'Why me, why me?' We say, 'Why you' as well. Why does dad come to him and not to us? It isn't fair.

This is another instance where a ghost appears to a complete stranger. Perhaps the ghost is there but only one person can see it. There have been several occasions when an apparition has appeared to a crowd of people. One or two see the ghost, a few just see a shape while others see nothing at all. There was, for example, a case at Kempsey in Worcestershire a few years ago when two ladies saw a Victorian farm labourer perched on a gate. The one lady simply saw a dark outline, while the other saw the ghost quite clearly. A third party might not have seen anything at all.

Scientists have proved that, in the same way that some people can hear wavelengths which are indiscernible to others, certain rays are visible to some and not others.

4. Birmingham West

A large part of the west and north-west of Birmingham, is occupied by the Black Country. However, also to the west are towns and villages such as Smethwick, Warley and Handsworth, who consider themselves to be quite separate from the Black Country. The author lived in Smethwick for many years and locals found it difficult to understand the Black Country dialect.

HANDSWORTH

As you drive round the insignificant roads of Handsworth, lined chiefly with late Victorian worker's houses, you would never guess that this was once one of the most exciting places in England. For in Handsworth, near the point where Hockley Brook is crossed by Factory Road, was The Soho Manufactory. It was founded by Matthew Boulton in 1762 for making buckles, buttons, plate and silverware using the latest technological advances and was the envy of Europe. He was a member of a group of intellectual inventors known as the Lunar Society. Another member was James Watt, who produced the steam engine which kick-started the industrial revolution. Matthew Boulton and James Watt went into partnership together.

The manufactory was the first building to use gas for lighting in 1802 or 3. The wattage measurement of lighting which every householder knows in the use of electric light bulbs, was been named after James Watt.

The Foundry was rebuilt in the 1860s and taken over by W & T Avery Ltd who were particularly famous for their weighing scales. The site is now covered by housing and the gardens cover such an important site that they have been excavated by the Channel 4 Time Team.

Unfortunately, no-one seems to have seen the ghost of Matthew Boulton or James Watt, but we do have two little stories for Handsworth.

Through the window!

Phillip now lives in Chase Town but when he was about six he used to live in an old Tudor House in Villa Road, Handsworth. He told this story on a programme with Dave Ellis.

> One night I woke up and I saw a lady at the foot of the bed. I had my godmother in bed with me at the time and she saw it as well. I got out of bed, put the light on and walked up to this lady. Off she went, straight through the window and we were about four stories up!
>
> Twenty-three years later, I went down to Wales where my godmother lived and asked her about it. She remembered it straight away. Neither of us have been able to explain it.

He seems to have been a very brave six year old! The sighting of ghosts has been attributed to your being half awake, when you think you are awake but are actually asleep and dreaming. If that is so, how can two people see the ghost? Are they both having the same dream?

Flippin' Heck!

On Hallowe'en 2002, Keith Middleton asked listeners to phone in with their ghost stories. One of the listeners was an elderly lady by the name of Millie:

> Last October my mother died in Barbados. At that time, I was living in Chester Road in Handsworth. I knew my mum was on her way out because she came into my bedroom at night. She looked like a young girl. I said, 'Flipping Heck, what are you doing here? You're not a young woman you know', and I was talking to her. I phoned my sister in New York and I said, 'Something's wrong, I'm sure my mum's not well' and I told her what had happened. She phoned home and the family told me that mum was seriously ill. The doctor said that he would give my mum until the Friday to die, but she didn't, she died on the Thursday.

SMETHWICK

An Arresting Tale

Ghosts wearing white macs are quite common, this is the fifth on our records. For example, just after World War II a lady in a white mac on a bicycle was seen many times on the road outside Coughton Court in Warwickshire, frightening motorists by jumping into the road.

> In the 1990s I was living in a block of flats in Smethwick. They had been built in the 1950s, my flat was on the top floor and my room was upstairs. I had a cat who would go and look up the stairs as if he was watching something. I kept having this feeling that I was being watched, and told my mate that I thought the flat was haunted. At about eight o'clock one summer evening, my mate was at work in the kitchen when he saw a figure in a white mac walk past the landing into the lounge. The cat looked up as well. My mate said, 'I think you're right, you know'.
>
> A year or two later another friend came and said to me, 'Can I go upstairs and use your phone?' I told him that of course he could. He was on the phone and when he looked in the mirror opposite he saw a figure come out of the wardrobe by the side of the phone and walk across the room and into the wardrobe the other side of the room. I said to him, 'What was this figure like?' He said it was wearing a white mac.

Later I discovered that the flats used to be Police Flats. You always think of a detective wearing a white mac, don't you?

By a strange co-incidence, the author's son lived in these flats during the 1990s but unfortunately never came face to face with an entity.

I Know What I Saw!

The author was educated (or otherwise) at Holly Lodge Girl's School in Smethwick. About a quarter of a mile south of the school, in a quiet residential area, is a three-bedroomed house occupied, in 1993, by Cynthia:

Somewhere between 10 and 12 o'clock I decided to go up to bed. My husband was sitting in the front room. I stood at the bottom of the stairs, looked up, and there at the top of the stairs was a ghost. I know it was there. I know it was a ghost. I know what I saw. It was a young man aged about 25 or 30 and he was all grey, with a grey top hat and grey cloak. He had no face, from his hat to his cloak was just a blank. I had the feeling he was at a party or something. As he stood there he tossed one end of his cloak over his shoulders. I can see it now in every detail.

I just stood there. I didn't know who it was. I know I saw it, I'm not crazy. I went into my husband and told him what I had seen. He looked at me for a minute or so and he said, 'Well, if you've seen it, that's it'. He never doubted my word. The strange thing is, I wasn't frightened of him. I just stood there and looked at him. I have often joked about it.

I only saw it once and I have never seen another ghost before or since. Somebody told us that there were just fields before the house was built in about the 1970s. Six months previously the house had been almost completely rebuilt. The house had been reduced to a shell, it had had a new roof and everything. We don't live there now.

Here is another 'pop-up' ghost. The lady who tells the story is sensible and intelligent, she was not half-awake, she is in perfect health, the house had no history and she had not been drinking. Yet she is adamant that she saw an apparition. The only comment we can make is that if radical changes are made to a house - if the house is damaged in any way - this very occasionally seems to release something from the woodwork. For example, a lady who lived in a beautiful half-timbered cottage in Henley-in-Arden had a chimney blown down through the roof. She had to sleep in another bedroom, and the first night there she saw a woman in an Elizabethan-type costume standing at the far side of the bed, leaning over her husband. He didn't see but he felt the apparition. However, the six months in the above story is an unusually long delay.

Many ghosts seem to be reluctant to reveal their features. Over and over again we have descriptions of ghosts where the faces are 'just a fuzz'. To take just one example, in 1975 Ann was driving home from Bromsgrove to Woolaston at one o'clock in the morning after a night out with her boyfriend, and when she had almost reached the Lydiate Ash motorway junction, a phantom horseman drifted across the road in front of her. She saw the white horse clearly and the clothes of the dark rider but his face was blurred.

Warley, West Smethwick

People taking their dogs for a walk in Warley Park and Lightwoods Park in the late evening might choose another venue if they knew the history of the area.

About 700 years ago, much of the land in Warley was held by Joan de Somery, who bequeathed her wealth to the monks of Halesowen Abbey on condition that they prayed eternally for her soul. Unfortunately, when Halesowen Abbey was dissolved by Henry VIII, there were no monks to continue the prayers. Joan appears to have made frequent visits to the park, perhaps to find out why her bequest was being ignored.

The grey lady paid so many visits to the park that in 1822 she was cited in a murder trial. The body of a man was found in the park, he had died from head injuries. Earlier in the day he had quarrelled with an acquaintance. The latter was charged with murder but stated that he was not to blame. He claimed that the deceased had been riding a horse which could have been startled by the appearance of the grey lady and thrown the rider. Three witnesses were produced who had seen the grey lady.

There are more sightings of the Warley ghost in *Strange Meetings*, published in 2002 by Quercus.

Oh, Not Again!

This is another of the stories told on Keith Middleton's programme in 2002. Lynne phoned in from Rowley Regis.

> When I was about fourteen or fifteen, which is going back a bit, me and my friend used to take short cuts over West Smethwick park, by the prefabs. One day, we saw a grey apparition sitting on the wall of the prefabs. They were warden-controlled, the warden came out, looked at the apparition and said, 'Oh no, not again'.
>
> The prefabs burned down the next day.

This incident attracted the attention of David Taylor, from Parasearch, who says:

> Ghosts that seem to be portents of future events are incredibly interesting. In the past such apparitions were often associated with large

country houses and the nobility. They were often seen as family ghosts, only appearing to warn of a coming death or disaster. It would certainly be interesting to find out if the ghost has been seen in the same area recently now that the prefabs have gone.

Come With Me

In May 2004 Danny Kelly invited phone-ins and Cyril from Warley told the following:

My mother died when I was only eighteen months old and I was brought up by my father and his sister. My dad was only a small man, about 5ft 3 but he was very strong and wiry. He worked on the railway and he always adored my mother. We were a large family but by the time I was 17 there was only my 20-year old brother and I left living at home, the others had married and gone away.

One night my brother and I had been to the pictures. We came home, we had a nice big fireplace and we sat one each side of the fireplace, as we often did, reading a book. At about half past eleven I went all queer and icy cold, so did my brother. We looked at each other.

Before my mother died, she had a cat that she was very fond of and she used to put it on her lap every night. This cat was still alive and was about twenty years of age. Suddenly the cat got up and started circling the centre of the room as if somebody was there and we could see the fur on her lying flat as if she was rubbing against somebody.

Now, my father got up promptly at seven o'clock every morning and the next morning he hadn't come down to make what he called his 'Manchester cup of tea' – just a plain cup of tea without sugar or milk. Evidently they had it like this in the railway. I said to my brother, 'Do you think we ought to wake him?' but my brother said to leave it. My father used to lock the door every night so that we couldn't just pop our head round the door. About 7.15 we heard the door go.

The kitchen was a kitchen-cum-breakfast room and the door to the stairs was on the right-hand side of the sink. I was just washing my hands when the door opened and when I saw dad I dropped the bar of soap. My brother said, 'What's the matter?' and I said, 'Just look at him'. When he went to bed he was a healthy man of 63 with black curly hair, now his eyes were sunk into the back of his head and he had gone white overnight. We said, 'What's the matter?' and he said, 'If I told you you wouldn't believe me. Your mother came to see me last night. She said, 'George, will you come with me, I want you?' There's an old saying that if you answer them you do go with them so I didn't answer.'

We asked him, 'What time was that?' and he said 'About halfpast eleven'. That was the time we felt all weird downstairs. Even now, when I think about it I feel queer.

Behold Thy Mother! – Quinton

Quinton is on the outskirts of the Birmingham conurbation and was in Worcestershire until 1909. Now it lies in the south western boundary of the West Midlands. It has been joined by junction 3 of the M5.

Roz from Quinton told this story to Ed Doolan one Bank Holiday Monday.

Many years ago I lived in a house where my mother and I had lived together but she had been dead for many years.

I had a veterinary surgeon who had a senior nurse called Shirley whom I knew professionally very well, but not personally. One day she rang me and asked if I would give a home to a kitten and I said that I would, so she brought him round. Three or four days later I rang the vet to say how the kitten was getting on and she invited me to go round for supper. So I went round and after the meal Shirley said to me, 'Can I ask you something Roz?' I replied, 'Of course you can'. She said, 'I don't want to upset you'. I said, 'Go on'. She said, 'Who was the lady standing at the bottom of your stairs when I called to bring the kitten to you?' I said, 'Go on'. She said, 'She was small, she had white hair done up in a roll at the back, she was wearing a purple dress and a purple amethyst oval brooch in a gold setting and a purple amethyst necklace, also with oval beads, and black shoes with a little bow on the side. Who was she, Roz?' I said, 'Shirley you have described my mother in her favourite outfit'. Now, I would like you to know that Shirley had never met my mother, we had never talked about her or anything else. But Shirley had seen her standing at the bottom of my stairs that day as clear as daylight.

We only knew each other professionally and the first time I knew her socially was when she invited me round for dinner that night to thank me for adopting the kitten. She had described my mother absolutely precisely but I couldn't see my mother. Roz said she was standing at the bottom of the stairs in the hall, absolutely motionless. She was there when she came in and she was there when she left.

5. Birmingham North

As the industrial revolution expanded, so the little villages surrounding Birmingham were swallowed up. In 1783 a history of Birmingham was published which stated that 'Birmingham is not a place gentlemen would chose to make a residence'. It was described as being overcrowded, smelly and full of smoke.

Bombed Out – Hockley

About a mile north from the city centre, is 'The Hockley Square Mile', better known as the jewellery quarter. The author worked in the jewellery quarter when in its heyday for seven years. It may now be quaint with many of the companies working there still using the traditional methods of their grandparents and even great-grandparents, but in its heyday it was overcrowded and sooty.

As part of industrial Birmingham, Hockley suffered badly in the last war, as Trevor's* story illustrates:

> In Cowper Street, Hockley, was an infants and Junior school which is where I went until I was about eleven, when I transferred to Summer Lane Secondary Modern.
>
> In about 1946, the war had been over for a year, and I was coming away from school in Summer Lane to my home in Cowper Street. On my way home I was approached by Mrs. Ingles. She was a little elderly lady whom I knew quite well because she was friend of my mother's. She stopped me and asked how my mother was and what my father was doing now that he had left the fire service. We had quite a nice little chat. We parted company and she turned into Ormond Street where she lived.
>
> I told my mother that I had just seen Mrs. Ingles. My mother looked rather ashen. She said, 'What do you mean, Mrs. Ingles?' I said, 'You know, Mrs. Ingles, your friend'. My mother asked me to describe her. Then she said, 'She couldn't possibly be Mrs. Ingles. She died a couple of years ago'. Towards the end of the war a bomb (I think it was a land mine) had fallen on Ormond Street and she was one of those who had been killed.
>
> It was quite an experience. I realised after that that I am sensitive to the paranormal, but that was the only time I have actually seen something. I was about 12 years of age and it was quite sobering. It just didn't seem to make sense to me. How could she be dead? I had just seen her.

This 'sensitivity' seems to take different forms. While some have the ability to see ghosts, others seem to be telepathic or can sense what has happened in the past, while yet others predict the future - a very useful expertise although no-one has yet claimed to have won the lottery by this ability!

The Dark Rider – Witton Cemetery

Running for about three-quarters of a mile close to the M6 as it leaves spaghetti junction is the huge Birmingham City Cemetery, the largest cemetery in England. The surrounding brick walls are two miles long. It was opened by Birmingham Corporation in 1863.

I think I have always had 'the gift'. I particularly remember one night, when I was about twelve, I was in bed but I couldn't sleep. All of a sudden I saw this shadow. I sat up in bed and my blood went to stone. I could see that it was the ghost of my grandmother, who had died the previous year. I was very close to my grandmother. She was dressed in white and her hair was brushed back, as she used to do it. Her face was as grey as anything. She just stood there, then she smiled at me and walked out through the wall. I was terrified.

My grandmother was buried in Witton cemetery in July 1980. I often went to visit her grave, but when I went in the January of the following year, I couldn't find it. There was ice and snow on the ground, it was about eight o'clock in the evening and very cold. All of a sudden, I heard a rumble and a motor bike came straight for me. The bike stopped and I stopped. It was a beautiful bike, all black and silver and the rider was wearing all black, black leather boots, black leather jacket and black helmet. His helmet was only about five inches away from me. He spoke to me through his helmet and asked me if I could find his girlfriend's grave. He said she had been killed in a motor bike accident. He was a really pleasant person, aged about nineteen or twenty. I said, 'I'm afraid I can't help you, I'm looking for my grandmother's grave'.

He turned round, I saw his red rear light for a second then he had gone. I had heard him approaching but I didn't hear him leave.

What makes me think it was a ghost is that it was late evening and the gates were locked. I had to climb over a high wall to get in, so how had he managed to get in? I thought at the time, 'That's a bit strange'. In later years said to myself, if he had come to visit the grave, where were his flowers?

This has stuck with me all through the years. I often wonder if he and his girlfriend had been in the same accident but the one had died before the other and they wanted to be reunited.

The Chairman of Parasearch, David Taylor, remarks:

Spectral figures mounted on a steed roaming among the dead – if it wasn't for the motorbike it could almost be the Wild Hunt! In many ancient cultures around the world the recently deceased are lead of an aerial flight lead by a spectral figure of supernatural origin. In Norse mythology the leader of the hunt was the god Woden, but he has many names. Maybe the Wild Hunt isn't as out dates as you think – maybe the hunter moves with the times!

A Sewing Machine Possessed – Sutton Coldfield

The prosperous part of the West Midlands is here. To the west is Sutton Park, the largest park in Birmingham, and to the east is farmland. Ruth's story shows that living in a privileged environment does not necessarily bring happiness:

Fifteen years last September my mother died. Let us say she was a very difficult woman, very domineering, and there were no tears shed. In her younger days she had been a dressmaker and a tailoress.

She died on the Thursday and my daughter was going on holiday the following Saturday. My daughter said, 'Oh dear, we hadn't better go now'. I told her, 'Don't cancel your holiday, Nanny's had her life, now you go and enjoy yours and we'll have the funeral afterwards'. Later that day, in the evening, I did a bit of sewing for my daughter, getting ready for the holiday, turning up the children's dresses and that kind of thing. I got my sewing machine out (an electrical one), put it on the table in the dining part of the kitchen and did the repairs.

I was sitting in the lounge about an hour-and-a-half later, watching T.V., when I suddenly heard a whirring sound. I thought, 'My goodness, what's that, is a kettle boiling over?' I went into the kitchen and there was the sewing machine, going all on its own, whirring away. I was quite shaken. I pulled the plug out of the wall. It was as if my mother was saying, 'You don't get rid of me that easily'. Of course, my husband had an explanation, he said that one of the little things in the pressure plate under the foot must have developed a fault, but it's never done that before or since.

There's a footnote to this. My mother was cremated at Sutton and it was a brilliantly sunny day, not a cloud in the sky. Yet as the coffin went down there was a tremendous rumble like a clap of thunder. My daughter nudged me and remarked afterwards, 'That sounded just like nanny'. We came out of the crematorium and there was still not a cloud in the sky.

The Disappearing Priest – New Oscott

New Oscott is a leafy village in the southern part of Sutton Coldfield. Ray* told this story on local radio:

I'm now going back about 70 years. When my mother was about nine years of age she was living in New Oscott. She was going home and there was a flood in the road. She was only small and she wondered how she was going to get across the water. She told us that a priest appeared quite suddenly out of nowhere, picked her up and carried her over the water. Then he suddenly disappeared. She said that there was something odd but unwordly about him, she was certain he was a spirit. There must have been some truth in her story because her feet were dry when she got home. There was a monastery nearby.

What a lovely, poetic story following in the great Christian tradition of helping travellers - here we have a twentieth-century Saint Christopher. There is an establishment for priests nearby, however it is not a monastery, but a college for the training of priests for England and Wales. It was founded in May 1794 at Oscott but outgrew the demand and was refounded at New Oscott in 1836. Among the architects and designers was the famous Augustus Pugin.

Lightning Strikes – Streetly

One of the largest parks in the West Midlands, if not the largest, is Sutton Park. Along its north western edge is the village of Streetly, situated on the line of the famous Roman Road, Icknield Street. However, Bob Smith's story is not a paranormal replay of ancient times but probably the result of a natural phenomenon:

> My wife and I had an experience in this house about ten or twelve years ago. I had taken her a cup of tea round about halfpast six or seven in the morning. She was sitting up in bed and I was sitting with my bum on the dressing table about twelve feet away, and we were talking. There was a thunderstorm going on, and all of a sudden, what I can only describe as a ball of orange fire, came through the window without breaking any glass. It was a little larger than a football, it looked solid, it did glow and in my mind's eye I think it was a bit feathered round the edges. There was no heat, no noise, no quivering sound, nothing. For a second or rather, a microsecond, it hung there suspended between the two of us. My mouth dropped open and bingo! it was gone. I think I'm right in saying that it went back out of the window again.
>
> After it had gone we just sat there with our mouths open, then I jumped up and inspected the window. There were no cracks, no scorch marks, no scratches, nothing.
>
> It set the alarms off, not only in this house but in five others alongside us as well. To turn the alarms off, we had to go back to the manufacturers for the code. There was a bloke down the road who fitted the alarms and he came and reset them for us. They were timed to go off and on for twenty minutes a time and they must have been going for a good hour.

This sounds like a case of 'ball lightning', well-known to meteorologists. A similar phenomenon is caused by escaping 'blobs' of gas from underground. In *Ghosts, Murders and Scandals (of Worcestershire),* Stella describes an incident which occurred when she and her husband were driving through the Lenches in Worcestershire at about nine o'clock one evening:

> It was just getting dark. My husband was behind the wheel. There was a light travelling behind us and getting closer and closer, it looked like the light of a motorbike until the light came through the back window, through the car and disappeared. My husband said, 'What was that?' He was really shaken. He had

to stop the car and walk up and down for a bit. I inspected the car but it hadn't done any damage.

A similar incident is recorded in Avon Dassett, when an object, about the size of a football and looking as if it was made from stainless steel was seen hanging in the sky before it moved sideways rapidly.

In *Midland Spirits and Spectres*, (published by Quercus in 1998), Barrie Roberts writes:

> The movement of underground rock formations creates electromagnetic 'blobs' that discharge into the atmosphere above ground. They appear only when the right kinds of rocks are moving, they glow in the dark, they hover and dart about and they shine in daylight.

6. The Black Country

Until medieval times the area north west of Birmingham was thinly populated and of no economic significance. It was mainly heathland, with poor soil and, with no rivers or main roads, access was difficult. From about the 1500s onwards everything changed. By 1850 it had become the most densely populated and economically vital part of the Midlands. It measured roughly ten by twelve miles and stretched from Wolverhampton and Walsall in the north to Stourbridge and Halesowen in the South. It became known as the Black Country. At night, the sky was red with the flames from the forges so that the Black Country was described as 'black by day and red by night'.

Coal, ironstone, clay, and lime were all readily available by mining and the many streams offered good sources of water power. Rods of wrought iron were smelted at local mills and thousands of smiths, working at open coal-fired hearths in little domestic workshops, converted them into nails, buckles, knives, locks, spurs and so on. The author's uncle lived in Halesowen in a large house surrounded by fields but at the bottom of his garden was a small brick building and round the walls were eight forges.

The Black Country was an area were men worked long hours for little pay, where smog and soot reigned, where poorly fed children died from consumption, smallpox, scarlet fever and a range of diseases unknown today. To those who have been bereaved, the possible visit of a deceased loved one can be a great comfort. These sightings are sometimes handed down through the generations until the loved one is forgotten and all that is left is the story of their ghost. Black Country people, like the Irish, have a love of story-telling. Perhaps is why, traditionally, the Black Country has more ghost stories than anywhere else in the Midlands.

The Malt Shovel – Blackheath

Ironworkers, especially those who work with an open forge, were thirsty men as their bodies ran with sweat all day and they needed to replace their fluids. Beer was usually the chosen drink. Wherever there were ironworkers, there would be a large number of public houses, especially after 1830 when the tax on beer was removed and the laws were changed so that anyone of good character could open a public house on payment of £2 2s.

Situated between Rowley Regis and Quinton, Blackheath is on the edge of the Black Country. Keith Middleton had a phone call from Lynne during one of his programmes in 2002:

> I used to keep the Malt Shovel in Blackheath on the High Street, opposite the George and Dragon. We had a spook in there. It used to turn the beer off. We had the old-fashioned pulls and the beer used to go off for no reason at all, it stopped

the water going and stopped the hosepipe going down the cellar.The doors used to slowly open and close, and cold shivers used to go up your spine. Even the men were afraid to stay in there.We used to have a guy who did relief and he used to stand on the doorstep and wait for somebody to come because he was so scared.

One evening I heard my son crying in his bedroom upstairs and so I went into his bedroom and he was as white as a ghost (oh, I shouldn't have said that should I!) – he was as white as a sheet. He'd got no breath at all, I had to run into the bedroom and shake him. He said that somebody had got their hands round his neck and was strangling him.There was no-one there at all.We think it was just a dream.

Sharon, the present licensee adds:

We haven't noticed any of Lynne's phenomena but we have experienced other things. We call our ghost 'George'. He likes to hide things – recently a bottle of Bacardi disappeared from one of the cellars then we found it two weeks later standing upright in the middle of another cellar. He does make a noise down the cellar. My office is upstairs and when I'm working I can hear him moving about down the cellar. There are strange noises and a rustling sound. I shout to him to be quiet until I've gone to bed!

DUDLEY

Right in the heart of the Black Country is the ancient town of Dudley. It developed around Dudley Castle, home of the mighty Dudley family. Among them was Elizabeth's favourite, Robert Dudley, Earl of Leicester.The castle was used as a Royalist stronghold in the Civil War and badly damaged in 1646.

The fifth baron Dudley had two families, his official family was in the castle but his favoured family lived in a cottage at the foot of the castle, where, say the locals, he spent most of his time. He looked after his illegitimate children well, sending his son, Dud Dudley to Oxford. Dud made the important discovery that coal could be used as a furnace fuel instead of charcoal.Although his experiments were not utilised during his lifetime, coal and its derivatives became the main fuel for furnaces. It was coal that added to the wealth of the Dudley family, they owned rich coal fields around Dudley. It has been said that so much coal has been mined from the hill on which Dudley Castle stands, that one day it will collapse.

Fogs and Orbs – Dudley Castle

Dudley Castle is teeming with ghosts. A miner was buried alive under a rockfall and the sound of his pick-axe can sometimes be heard at night. The Under-Manager of the ballroom was confronted by a white luminous figure. One evening, two young entertainers saw the dark hazy shape of a woman on the castle mound. Near to the castle are the ruins of St. James' Priory, founded in

A guy walked down the path towards us, pretending to be one of the historical characters, he had got a wonderful mask on... there was something like a small fog coming across.

the late 1100s and from time to time a dark monk wanders round the castle. A young man on a paranormal investigation was going up a flight of stairs when he was lifted into the air and tossed down the staircase. The investigation had to be abandoned. At a fancy dress party, judges decided to award a prize to an authentic-looking medieval lady but when the prizes were presented, she had disappeared despite strict security.

During a programme when Dave Ellis was standing in for Ed Doolan, Kate Walker gave an account of her experience on the Ghost Walk.

> It's very well done. You walk round the place and they say, this is what happened here and this is allegedly what is going to happen. Things jump out at you. My little relative was with me, she didn't realise that the ghosts all around us were actors and she was screaming her head off, bless her, so she was doing some entertainment of her own. A guy walked down the path towards us pretending to be one of the historical characters, he had got a wonderful mask on so I took some photographs using a digital camera. At the time I thought, 'That's weird', because there was something like a small fog coming across, then I took another one and it was clear. My finger wasn't in the way of the camera lens and I wasn't smoking. I took another photo, the fog had gone but there were little circles of light – I think they call them light orbs, around this guy. I took a final photo and that was completely clear. It was really weird.
>
> I didn't think much of it but afterwards, when we walked back to the pub, I told the guide and he said that that had happened before in that place and with that actor. It's almost as if something is centred at that one spot.

If you have a fine water spray and aim it so that a drop or two lands on the lens of your digital camera, you will find that your next photograph has 'orbs' on it. Why this should happen on digital cameras rather than conventional cameras is anyone's guess. You will notice that the edges of the orbs are blurred, showing that the orb was very close to the camera lens.

Occasionally, orbs have been seen before a photograph was taken, in which case the orbs should have hard edges and the Midland paranormal society, Parasearch would love to hear about it. They can be contacted at david.taylor@parasearch.org.uk.

Since 1995, Parasearch has been involved in a detailed investigation of Dudley Castle. Through the kind and invaluable assistance of Adrian Durkin, they have monitored the castle, spoken to witnesses and examined photographs. Their official report says, 'Without doubt, unusual things have been experienced here'.

The Strange Tale of Melissa

Melissa finds her 'gift' embarrassing and a nuisance. A few years ago she was having a problem with migraines and taken into a neurological hospital. While she was there the hospital staff discovered that she was telepathic. She could tell the doctors what they were thinking and was able to describe the contents of their pockets. She was sent for tests but withdrew because 'I was fed up of being treated like a prize guinea pig'. Melissa has been persuaded to describe one of her experiences:

> About eight years ago a friend of mine was admitted to Burton Road Hospital, Dudley. I went to visit him and as I drove towards the entrance of the hospital I could see that there had been an accident. One car, I think it was dark blue, was very badly mangled. Two men were shouting at each other. One was wearing a maroon sweater with a shirt underneath and silvery-grey trousers – he was shouting the loudest – and the other was wearing a bomber jacket. The one was standing on the pavement while the other was standing on the road with his hand on the car. There was glass and metal everywhere, all over the road. I drove into the hospital and discovered that my friend had been discharged, so I turned round and drove out. This could have taken no longer than about three minutes. I thought, 'I must drive carefully as I go out to avoid the glass'. I got to the end of the drive and there was no glass – nothing. Some people were waiting for the bus nearby so I wound down the window and asked them what had happened to the accident. They looked at me as if I was some kind of imbecile. It frightened me.

The Death Rattle

We have met the highly qualified George Gregg before (MSc, MA, CertEd), the Research Officer for the paranormal investigative group, Parasearch. He has had a number of unusual experiences himself which he tries to analyse from both a paranormal and scientific aspect. The following are his first two personal experiences and there will be others in the Worcestershire chapter.

> In 2004, a Psychical Research team with which I was involved, were carrying out ghost vigils at a Higher Education establishment in the Dudley Area. As usual with this kind of thing, phenomena was at a low level. However, I was with a group sitting quietly by a lift. My professional experience is that of nursing and this is why, about ten minutes before the end of our 4.00 am vigil, I heard a loud expiration of air. Normally I would have put it down to noises from the lift but the sound that came with it was recognisable. I heard an intake of breath with a crepitus, (a crackling sound, similar to that heard through a stethoscope over an inflamed lung when a patient has pneumonia or similar disease). The problem was that I heard it, so did another person, and we only heard it once. Had it been the lift, we should have heard it several times.
>
> *Paranormal explanation:* A sound being replayed from the past of a sick old codger breathing out.
>
> *Scientific Explanation:* The settling of the mechanics of the lift or ventilation system that mimics the sound of a crepitus/expiration of breath.

Haunted Hooves – Oldbury

Oldbury goes back to the 1200s but, with its natural deposits of coal and iron, it started to expand in the 18th century when canals reached its doors. This is the second of George Gregg's experiences, this time in an ever-popular public house:

I was with a group of psychical researchers in a pub near Oldbury in 2000. We had carried out our investigations throughout the night with no avail. It is often the case that there is little of the paranormal to report. However as I was packing my equipment away I heard the noise of horses hooves. Of course, it was getting light at the time and I gave it little thought except to say that I was going to keep my eye open as I was leaving the pub in case I spooked the horses by driving my car out in the dim light. However I pulled out of the drive, after having wished my colleagues the best, and the horses went completely out of my mind.

I discovered a fortnight later at a group meeting that there are no horse or stables nearby and that one of the ghostly phenomena at the pub was that a spectral coach and four pull in from time to time.

Paranormal Explanation: This could be an example of stone tape theory where some aspect of the past has been recorded in the environment, such as the pub's outside walls, and has been activated by some as yet unknown stimulus. Sometimes the sound is played, sometimes the pictures (holographic universe theory) or both.

Psychological explanation: There could have been some other sound in the environment that my brain interpreted as the noise of horses hooves.

The Old Couple – West Bromwich

Since the 17th Century, when, West Bromwich has been an industrial town. First it was a town of nailers and buckle-makers, later it became famous for its springs and enamelled holloware. In June 2006, the popular radio presenter, Danny Kelly, asked for ghostly tales and Dave phoned with a touching story about his grandparents:

Both my grandfather and grandmother were born and bred in West Bromwich, my grandfather was born in Spon Lane in 1898. There were mines all over the place, he was an old miner and I remember him telling me that all Kelvin Way used to be old mine workings. Like all miners, my grandfather was very superstitious. He once saw a black cat on his way to work so he turned round and went home. My grandmother was superstitious too, I used to get into trouble for doing things like spinning knives on the dining table.

They had been happily married for more than 50 years when my grandfather died suddenly in 1971. They were living in a flat on the Yew Tree Estate. My grandmother was a diabetic and she had been resting on her bed, waiting for the nurse to come and give her an injection. Grandmother got off the bed and went to get into the sitting room but she was nearly blind and couldn't open the door. She managed to scramble to the front door to meet the nurse coming up the drive. When the nurse opened the door she found that my grandfather had died in his armchair.

My grandmother went to live with her daughter a few houses away. While she was living there, she had occasion to go to the bathroom in the night. As she went across the landing she saw my grandfather standing at the top of the stairs with his arms outstretched, evidently to prevent her falling down the stairs. He said, 'Come on, my wench, you will be alright while I'm here'. Then he added, 'Never mind my love, we shall soon be together again'. She told my father and he just remarked that she had been half asleep or something but within twelve months she herself had passed away.

This is a lovely example of the way in which ghost stories preserve history. What a pity the old couple have not put on record all their memories before they passed away. Quite apart from the old mine workings and the superstitions, in ten years time perhaps no-one will need an injection of insulin! With these stories we're capturing many aspects of our present-day life.

WEDNESBURY

The name 'Wednesbury' is significant for it means 'the defended place of Woden'. He was the chief of the Anglo-Saxon Gods, so that we know that the town is a thousand years old or so and that its inhabitants worshipped pagan gods. The forging of metals was first recorded here at the Wednesbury Forge in 1597.

The Old Patrick Bar

Dawn worked at the Old Patrick bar for many years. Unfortunately, it closed in about 2005.

The first time I saw the young man was last winter. We had had a party in the night club the night before and I was tidying up. I went along one of the corridors and he was standing there. All the doors were locked, so nobody could have got in. You could see him so clearly! He looked solid, just as if I was talking to you. He was about 20 with dark hair, average height and build, he wore blue jeans, a shirt in a light colour and there was blood down the left hand side of his face. He had got a bottle of beer in his hand. He was talking but he was mumbling and it was nothing that I could understand. He was there for about a minute. To be quite honest, I felt like running home.

I saw him at least 15 or 20 times in all. He appeared in different places but I only ever saw him in the night club, never in the pub. He always stood still. The first two or three times I saw him I was really scared, then it came so that I took no notice, I just carried on working. I tried talking to him but he only mumbled.

I didn't believe in ghosts before then. If you had told me about a ghost I would have said,'pull the other one, it's got bells on it'. Other people saw him as well: a member of the bar staff and a manager before my time. He first appeared in about 1999.

The strange thing was a young man died there about five years ago. The bouncers threw him out, he went outside, a fight continued and this guy got fatally injured. They carried him into the club where he died.

Remember the 'stone tape' theory? Some paranormal enthusiasts believe that when a tragic event occurs, such as a murder, it leaves what is known as 'an impression on time' which can be picked up later, perhaps years or centuries in the future, by a sensitive person. Did this murder leave an impression on time? The blood on the face seems significant.

The Ghost Throws Toilet Rolls

There's an old Picture House on the Old Walsall Road in Wednesbury which is now a Bingo Hall. A local resident says that several peculiar things have happened on a number occasions.

The wife has worked there for 20 or more years. The most active time was when it was being refurbished. A lot of cleaners left because they were tapped on the shoulder and that sort of thing.

When it was being refurbished the Hall was left open and there were no alarms, so the workers had to take it in turns to keep watch there all night. One chap was really tough, but at two o'clock in the morning he rang the wife up and told her that he couldn't stay there any longer. I had to go and take over. I took my Labrador and looked round the building to see if anyone had got in. The Labrador kept howling terribly, especially when we went up the balcony. There are cold spots here and there and you can also smell tobacco smoke in places.

The ghost has been throwing toilet rolls. The wife opened up the old cinema for a delivery of toilet rolls. The wife and the driver stacked them up across the bottom of the hall. They went away then when they came back the toilet rolls had been thrown all over the hall. The driver said, 'Who has got in here?' They stacked the toilet rolls up and again, when they returned, the rolls were all over the hall.

I was a sceptic until a few years ago when all this happened.

The Haunted Cat – Bilston

A whole book could be written about the ghosts and legends of Bilston. A coalmine here had an appalling record of accidents in the 17th and 18th centuries. As we have seen in Dave's story, about his grandparents, the miners were superstitious and would not go to work if, for example, they saw a black cat or heard a flock of geese flying overhead. Bilston mine was considered to be 'unlucky' so the story goes that the local white witch was called in to change the luck. He told a group of men to visit the mine at midnight and the leader, Caggie, was to hold a Bible in his right hand and a key in his left, while they all chanted, 'Matthew, Mark, Luke and John, God bless the errand we've come on' and they were to repeat the Lord's Prayer backwards. The men carried out the instructions but down the mine, they saw, in front of them, a large white ghost. The ghost advanced, ignoring their chants. Suddenly, someone realised that 'Caggie' means left-handed and yelled out, 'Caggie, put the book in yer right 'and'. Caggie did so and the ghost disappeared.

Barrie Roberts adds that 40 years ago, while working in a mining town in Scotland, he heard the same story, though the Scottish 'hero' was called 'Cocky'.

Bilston had the reputation of a hard-drinking town and the most popular public house, the 'Lamb and Flag' was known locally as 'The Hell Hole'.

Some of the old iron workers and iron masters were reluctant to change to other occupations. Bilston was a town that clung to its ancient traditions to the last, with a blast furnace continuing well into the 1970s using imported iron ores.

Josephine lives in Bilston but sometimes her work takes her into Bloxwich, and it was on a drive home one night that she had a curious experience:

> I used to be a community worker and the things I used to see at night, they were remarkable! But one night, about half eleven or twelve o'clock, when I was coming home from the Bloxwich area, I saw a little cat sitting on the pavement. I thought, 'Oh, I hope he doesn't run into the road'. When I got near it my car went over something. Stupidly, I got out to look to see if the cat was injured, but there was no cat near. I got down to the traffic lights and I was surprised to see it standing there, looking at me. That cat followed me for about six miles until I got home. Every time I passed by I could feel that I would go over something. Every time I got to any traffic lights it was waiting for me. When I got home it was sitting on the pavement across my house. Then it disappeared.

When she told Ed Doolan about the incident on local radio in 2002, he remarked that it was a very curious story, quite unlike any that he had previously heard.

Terrified Motorists – Himley Hall

If you wish to follow in the footsteps of royalty, to dine where lords and ladies enjoyed their repasts or wander on a green once the haunt of princes and earls, then this is the venue for you.

Himley Hall is just outside Wolverhampton and was originally a medieval moated manor house belonging to the Earls of Dudley. In 1740, it was decided to replace it with a Palladian mansion. The 180 acres of parkland was designed by Capability Brown who created the great lake. In the 1920s and 30s it was the haunt of Royalty, and the Duke and Duchess of Kent spent the first two weeks of their honeymoon here. Edward VIII, Duke of Windsor, sought solitude here on the last weekend before his abdication. In 1966 Himley Hall was purchased by Dudley and Wolverhampton District Councils and opened as a public leisure area. It is now a Conference and Events Centre. The present warden says:

> Himley Hall is surrounded by a park in which are two sets of gates, the west gate and the east gate. On the other side of the road, midway between the two, is Home Farm. In its heyday, there were 141 staff at Himley Hall and some of these staff lived at Home Farm. There was a gate set in the fencing opposite Home Farm so that they could easily walk to and fro between the Hall and the Farm.
>
> I have been here for nineteen years and during my time here on at least five occasions a motorist has swerved and gone into the fence where the old gate once existed. The explanation is always the same, the motorist says that a 'strangely attired' girl in a floor-length dark grey dress suddenly walked out into the road, yet when the driver jumps out of the car, nobody is around. They are confused, traumatised and shaken up. All you can get from them is that they swerved to avoid a 'funny woman'. Only the driver sees her, not the passenger.
>
> From their description and piecing together various bits of information we surmise that this was a senior servant girl who lived at the farm and worked at Himley Hall during the early Victorian period. She has apparently been running across the road for about 150 years!
>
> Because of the renowned Himley Bonfire and Fireworks display and other large scale events staged in the park, we needed to create an additional gateway onto the road opposite the access drive to Home Farm. This was done by replacing two sections of fencing which can now easily be opened and utilised as gates. That was done in 1994 and since then the servant girl has not been seen.
>
> We also have a soldier from Charles I's army. King Charles stayed here in 1645 before the battle of Naseby and the army camped in the grounds. Afterwards there was a mutiny – the details have been documented in diaries. The leader was court-martialled, hanged and buried here. This upset him and ever afterwards he has appeared in the park in the evening. He has been seen at least three times to my knowledge during my time here, principally by the Night Syndicate Fishing members. Mind you, I don't know how much they had been drinking!

Naseby is about seven miles from Market Harborough. The king had an army of about 7,500 men but the Parliamentarians under Fairfax and Cromwell had about 13,000. Charles lost most of his army in the battle, about 1,000 were killed and 5,000 were taken prisoner. He fled to Leicester.

In November 1605, the gunpowder plotters were captured after a bloody battle in nearby Holbeach House. According to local tradition, a young groom, Gideon Grove managed to escape in the dust and confusion but was captured in Himley Wood. Now, once a year, his ghost rides through the wood, chased by a red-coated posse.

The Old Stag's Head – Penn Common

Near Dudley and Wolverhampton, between the A449 to the west and the A459 to the east, is a great swathe of green, Penn Common and Buggeridge Wood. (Only the Black Country would have a wood called, 'Buggeridge'.) Off the A449 and leading on to Penn Common is Church Hill and at the bottom of this road is The Old Stag's Head. Marlene has been licensee for 29 years and in June 2006, she telephoned Danny Kelly, the popular presenter, to say that her pub was haunted:

> The pub goes back to 1870 but it's a bit like the Marie Celeste, it's disappeared without trace from the records. It's not mentioned in any of them. There are no pictures, nothing. Recently a plan of the town was made for Millennium Place and every pub in the town was on it but not ours. I have been into Stafford to try and find out its history but can't find anything. Last year I had a telephone call from a lady who said that she used to live here and she would call in and tell me about it but I never heard from her again. I was so disappointed. Perhaps she'll read this and come forward.
>
> Our pub backs on to the churchyard. Between us and the church is a little cottage that I'm told was once part of the pub – an old coaching inn, then a house, then the church.
>
> I'm told that, many years ago, the vicar used to pop in here for a drink before, after or during the service. His wife said that one day, she would come in and turn the beer off. We came here a month before I had my second baby. My husband had gone out, he was taking a retired licensee home, and I was working behind the bar with my brother when he suddenly said, 'The beer's not coming through'. I told him, 'It must be working, I've spent the last two hours cleaning it'. We went through every pull on the counter and none of them worked. I said to him, 'Come down the cellar with me in case the barrels need changing' – they're heavy those barrels and I was very pregnant. We went down the cellar and all the taps had been turned off. No-one had been down there. Now, you tell me who could have done that?
>
> We have a traditional ghost here, she's always been known as 'the white lady'. When we came here, my elder daughter, Charlotte, was three years old. She didn't know what a ghost was. At nights, when she was in bed, we could hear her talking to someone. Sometimes she came into our bed for a cuddle and she would say, 'I'm talking to the lady'.

Strange things have happened many, many times. I have had my name called. I have heard someone walking across the landing. Doors open slowly and then close. Our cleaner can hear people talking and doors opening and shutting. I saw her cleaning in the bar one day then suddenly she disappeared. I thought she must be in the garden. I walked round the bar and there she was, lying on the floor. She said, 'A woman has just walked right the way through me'.

I have got a £3,000 diamond ring which I always kept in the same place, in a drawer in my bedroom. I was sitting on the settee in the living room when a voice in my head said to me, 'Go and look for the ring'. It wasn't there. I turned everything out but I couldn't find it. I panicked, I fetched my husband and he turned everything out. I have a friend who comes and she brings her little girl who sometimes plays with the things in my bedroom. I went to see her and asked if her little girl had been playing with the ring, but she hadn't. I got back home and I thought, 'What am I going to do?' Then a voice came into my head again, 'Go and look for the ring'. I got up and went to look for it, opened the drawer and there it was, right in front of me.

A young girl came to help behind the bar and her brother was in a psychic circle or something. She asked if he could come upstairs into our private apartment. He went upstairs where I was sitting on the settee with my cocker spaniel. He said, 'You have got your ghost'. I asked him what he meant. He said, 'She's standing behind you and smiling, she's saying, 'Thank you for all the improvements you have made to the premises'. She is here to protect you. She walks into every room before you do to make sure it's safe'.

Me and my daughter went into Birmingham to do some shopping and went into Rackhams. One of the assistants – we have never seen her before – she came from another department and said to us, 'You have got two ghosts in your house. One is female and she protects you from the other ghost, who is a malevolent male'. It's funny she should say that. Two years ago I was in bed and I felt someone come up the side of the bed and put his hands round my neck. I had to force his hands away. I had the marks on my neck afterwards.

My one daughter won't stay in the house on her own. The cellar is the worst part. The dogs are petrified and won't go down the cellar but they sit by the cellar door, growling. Our cook's son went to the toilet and came out absolutely petrified. He said a dark shape was standing next to him. That wouldn't have been the white lady, of course.

As soon as we set off on holiday everything starts breaking down – the equipment, the lights start cracking etcetera. The staff say that the ghost doesn't want me to leave. When I get back the staff say, 'You wouldn't believe what's been happening here'. We call the white lady, 'Wendy', and I say, 'Goodbye Wendy, I'll be back soon'. I feel that I have a companion in her.

> I'm not frightened, it's lovely here. It's a Victorian pub and it's like going back in time. We have large paintings as they did in those days, and our furnishings are Regency and Victorian. It always gives good vibes.

WOLVERHAMPTON

Wolverhampton is a curious mixture of ancient and modern. It has the 13th century church of St. Peter ('modernised' by the Victorians) with a famous cross shaft dating back to the 12th century, but set against these is an enormous covered shopping centre and the terminus of the Metro. The town has been famous for its metalwork, especially locks and keys, and in the late 16th and early 17th century 22 percent of the inhabitants were metalworkers. Wolverhampton was well-known for the repair sheds of the Great Western Railway and many a famous engineer learned his trade there, such as Robert Walker Smith who developed the Royal Enfield motor bikes.

The Phantom Lorry

Although Susan now lives in Ludlow, she used to live in Wolverhampton.

> Every afternoon I collected my two boys from School. The following incident occurred late one winter afternoon when it was almost dark and I was driving along Castlecroft Lane, by the Staffordshire and Worcester Canal, with my seven year old in the front with me and the five year old in the back.
>
> Suddenly, I saw the lights of a lorry approaching. There wasn't room for the two of us to pass so I stopped and drew into the side as much as possible. To my horror, the lorry came straight on. I saw it clearly, it was a square-shaped lorry, one of the old-fashioned kind. I said to the boys, 'Hold on, we're going to crash' but the lorry came straight through us. I sat there, astonished. I said to the boys, 'Did you see that?'

There's an excellent 'phantom lorry' story in Betty Smith's book, *Hidden Warwickshire*. In Ryton-on-Dunsmore, a number of vehicles collided on an icy road on a bend. To warn oncoming traffic, the single policeman on the scene and a helper lit a bonfire in the middle of the road. A lorry came whizzing round the corner and drove straight through the scene, flames and all. Onlookers realised that they could see through the sides of the lorry.

David Taylor of Parasearch says:

> Ghosts of cars and lorries are a modern version of the phantom coach and horses. There are reports of a ghost lorry near Rugby and even a spectral bus in Kensington! If ghosts are spirits of the dead, how do we explain ghosts of inanimate objects? Many researchers believe that events can be 'recorded' onto the environment like a tape recording onto magnetic tape. Perhaps this goes some way to explaining reports like this.

The Coach Driver's Story

There are innumerable stories for ghosts on roads. In *Haunted Holidays* there is a whole chapter on 'Phantoms of the Road'. A man fell in front of a lorry near Carmarthen, but when the lorry driver turned round and went back, nothing was there. A mother and son travelling up to Scotland one dark night both saw a lady whose head was lit up like a balloon. A young businessman from Stratford-on-Avon glimpsed part of a coach and horses before they disappeared.

This is another of Barry the Blacksmith's tales and comes from the time that he was working as a coach driver at a depot not far from Wolverhampton:

> Harry Hall and I were both coach drivers for a well-known Midlands company. He was one of the best drivers I ever knew and well-liked by passengers and colleagues. So, despite being pleased when I was told that I was going on a long-distance breakdown to South Moulton in Devon, I was dismayed to learn that it was Harry's coach that had gone off the road.
>
> I arrived at the scene some hours later and in daylight. The coach had gone through a hedge, narrowly missing a large tree, and down an embankment. No other vehicle was involved. My mate and I pulled the coach out of its predicament fairly easily, suspended it from the crane at the back of the recovery vehicle and towed it back to the Midlands.
>
> Because of our involvement with the accident, my mate and I followed the subsequent inquiry with interest. As I said, no other vehicle was involved in the accident, and investigation proved that there was nothing amiss with the steering or brakes of the coach. The only remaining possibility was driver error, so the inquiry determined.
>
> Some time later I bumped into Harry, he was a shadow of his former self. The first and most obvious sign of his ordeal was his hair, from being almost black-haired he had become pure white. The man was stooped when he had been upright and his hands trembled constantly. This is what he told me:
>
> He had been travelling south, he knew the road well and was aware of the bend going into the market town of South Moulton. He estimated that he was travelling at forty miles an hour, the enquiry confirmed this, perfectly safely. As he was braking into the bend Harry realised that another coach, travelling in the opposite direction was coming straight at him on his side of the road. Harry instinctively swerved to avoid the oncoming coach.
>
> On this occasion there was no other coach, extensive inquiries had proved this. However, two years to the day previously, there had been another coach which had crashed on that corner with considerable loss of life. Fortunately Harry's passengers only sustained minor injuries. Harry himself came off worst, he was injured by flying glass and never drove again.

In *Haunted Holidays*, David Taylor writes,

Ghosts of the road, whether they be the archetypal phantom coach and horses, headless horsemen or the more modern phantom hitchhiker, have a long and ancient tradition. They are even given their own section in the Folklore Motif-Index used by professional folklorists.

The Lord is My Shepherd

Debbie from Wolverhampton told this story on Keith Middleton's show in 2002:

I do think that children are open to everything. When I was little, there weren't such things as telephones – well there were, but only rich people had them. My uncle lived in the Welsh valleys and I told my mum that he had died. She said, 'You shouldn't say things like that'. The following morning we had a telegram to say that he had died.

I also told my mum the night her mum had died, and she had. I was nineteen and although my nan was in New Cross Hospital, I woke up in the night to find her sitting in my bed, singing 'The Lord is my shepherd'. It didn't frighten me at all. What is there to be frightened of? They can't hurt you.

Are children more spiritually sensitive than adults? Various experiments have been carried out which suggest that children tend to be quite telepathic but grow out of this as they mature. *Haunted Holidays* has a whole chapter on childhood experiences. David Taylor asks,

Is this the natural consequence of growing up or is it the result of the pressures of society? Our aim is to see our children growing up as sensible, achieving adults. We encourage them to work hard, we don't like to see them idle or 'messing about'. We dismiss as ridiculous anything which does not fit in to our logical understanding. ... Perhaps it is not so much that children have the ability to believe, rather they have not learned to doubt!

Most people have heard of a situation where someone has been visited by an apparition of the dead or dying. The paranormal researcher and lecturer, Barrie Roberts, says that when the exact times are compared, it's usually found that the apparition appears just before death. This suggests that the dying individual has been thinking about that person, who perhaps picks up those thoughts with a telepathic image.

Spirits of a Different Kind

Dave Ellis was hosting a phone-in when he heard the following from Wolverhampton-based Kevin:

I have been interested in the paranormal since I was 9 years old. and I'm now 41. I have had a number of strange experiences. I just can't explain them myself.

My earliest ghost experience was when I was 16. I was working as an apprentice plumber at Wolverhampton Brewery (Banks's), but I hadn't had a drink or anything at the time. We were just doing general piping work for the Brewery.

In one area we had got our tools for the blockupping. I was down there one day, getting some stuff out, and I saw a guy in an overall bib and braces type of thing. He was wandering round by our tools and I thought, 'Oh Christ, I'm in charge of these', – being 16 and a young apprentice, you're in charge of the tools. Anyway, I just went to see what was going on and this guy walked round the back of a tank. I followed him, just to make sure that he hadn't pinched any of our tools. I walked round the back – gone, nothing. The tanks were on solid brick plinths, there was no crawl space, anything like that, and I had got a solid brick wall facing me I couldn't explain it.

Some of the other guys had various paranormal tales to tell but they came from different places in the Brewery.

It would be interesting to hear Kevin's other experiences.

The Rippling Bed

Trevor says that his story goes back 30 years as his daughter is 33 now and she would have been about three at the time.

We lived in Wolverhampton in one of the flats built on the site of some old hostels. It was a two-bedroomed flat, you went in the front door, the staircase was in front of you and you went straight into the main bedroom. To the left was the bathroom and you would double back on yourself for the single bedroom.

At first, a few strange things happened but we didn't think anything about them. The first thing was that we had some friends in, and when my friend's wife got half way down the hall she stopped and shuddered. We asked, 'What's the matter?' She said, 'There's a cold spot in your hall'.

My daughter started screaming in the night, and it wasn't the normal cry of a child, she sounded terrified. Then one night, my daughter was crying in the small bedroom, so I picked her up, put her in with my wife, and got into her single bed. As soon as I lay down I felt the bed rippling under me. You know the wave machines that you get sometimes, it was just like that. I jumped out of bed and looked at the bed but the rippling had stopped. I spoke out loud, 'Now come on, you're a rational, level-headed man' and I got back into bed again. As soon as I was back in bed, the rippling started again. I just lay there until it stopped, it went on for about fifteen or twenty minutes.

On another occasion my wife went out for the evening with her mum and I was doing the baby sitting. When I got to the bottom of the stairs I looked up as you do and heard what I can only describe as a wind funnel, with all sorts of noises and the muffled sounds of people talking. It lasted several minutes.

Periodically my wife used to sit up in bed and look at the door then her eyes would follow something moving across the bedroom. She said there was an old man with a basket going across the bedroom but I couldn't see anything.

I was on shifts so my wife used to wake me up about five o'clock in the evening with a cup of coffee. One evening, she left the bedroom door open and through the door I saw a dark shape of something like an old sack hunched over, going from left to right. I called out, 'Has anybody come upstairs?' and my wife said, 'No, why do you want to know?' and I said, 'It doesn't matter'. I went into the spare bedroom to check and nobody was there. I'm getting the hairs on the back of my neck standing up while I'm telling you this. I never said anything to the wife as she was alone at nights and I didn't want to frighten her.

By this time, I was thinking, I shall be glad to get out of here, and we put in for another flat. In the meantime, the lady next door was moving out and so we went round to say goodbye. She said, 'Between you and me I shall be glad to get out of here. You may not believe this but there's a man walks through the wall adjoining your flat into ours'.

As soon as we moved my daughter stopped screaming at nights. I'm a sensible, level-headed man and I have never experienced anything strange before or since. I know it wasn't my imagination. What happened to me was really weird.

The flats have now been pulled down.

We have several instances where a ghost walks through a wall and comes out the other side. A six-year old daughter in Merry Hill kept complaining that a man came into her bedroom at night. The mother 'pooh-poohed' the story until she was lying in bed one night and a dark figure walked out of the adjoining wall!

Forgotten Slippers

RAJ was born and bred in England but his parents come from India:

If you go on holiday to India and stay with a relative, when you get back to England, you always have to send the host something as a 'thank you'. My mum went to India and she stayed at her sister's house. Her sister said, 'Please could you send me a pair of slippers?' Anyway, mum forgot.

After some time, her sister died – she was stung in the foot by a scorpion. A few weeks later, my mum said to us, 'Take me to the shoe shop'. We asked her why, and she said that she wanted to buy some slippers. We said, 'You already have slippers' but she told us that her sister had come to her in a dream and said, 'You promised me a pair of slippers. Where are they?' Mum bought the slippers and gave them to the temple.

His Come-uppance

Anyone with a 'difficult' father-in-law will enjoy the next tale:

This is my second marriage, consequently, although I am in my fifties I have parents-in-law who are in their nineties. They were doing well until about 18 months ago when mum was taken poorly. She didn't want to go into hospital so my husband asked me if we could nurse her at home. I used to be a nurse, so I said, 'Of course'. She was a lovely lady. I looked after her for the two weeks before she died.

The only trouble was that we had to have her husband as well and he was a cantankerous old man. He had had his wife running round him from five in the morning until late at night. During the two weeks she was at my house, I caught him taking her rings off. I said to him, 'What are you doing?' He said, 'I've promised her rings to Stella (his other daughter) and I want to make sure she gets them!' Another day he said to me, 'Go down now and get her pension before she dies!' After the two weeks we transferred her to Selly Oak hospital where she died the same day.

Strange things concerning mum have happened to my step-daughter and myself. For example, my step-daughter is in Australia and she had a watch that used to belong to mum. She had it for 36 years without a problem but the day that mum died, the watch stopped.

Towards Christmas we went to see my father-in-law and he said, 'I've told the neighbours I'm coming to you for Christmas'. My daughter came to stay with us as well. While she was taking the presents round the neighbours, I packed the old man off to bed. The next morning he came down and he was as white as a sheet. I asked him, 'Didn't you have a good night's sleep?' and he said, 'It's freezing in my room'. I pointed out that the central heating had been on all night. He replied that the quilt kept falling off.

He couldn't get out of our house quick enough. He wouldn't stop for his Christmas breakfast or his presents or anything. We had to run him home straight away.

This puzzled me, as I had put him in a single bed and given him a double quilt. How could the quilt have kept falling off during the night? Also, when I went into his room the radiator wasn't working. A short while after he left, it started working again and warmed up. I have never known that radiator to go wrong before and it hasn't gone wrong since. I think something happened to him that night and he got his come-uppence.

Lost and Found – Walsall

Walsall was once famous for its saddlery equipment including spurs, stirrups and other saddlery irons, and, as most transport was by horse until the Second

World War, it became an important and prosperous town. This is a town that once had the reputation of housing a large number of under-privileged folk but is managing to turn its reputation round. It now has a Museum of Leather and has even acquired an art gallery of international renown.

Local folklore recorded in the nineteenth century states that St. Matthew's church was moved to its present site by fairies. The site originally chosen for the church was at Chuckery, one of the suburbs of Walsall, but for some reason the fairies didn't like this, and so moved it to its present position. Charles Poole, recorded this story in the 1880's in his *Customs, Superstitions and Legends of Stafford*. He wrote 'The vicinity is, according to popular belief, peopled by the little folk who still gambol there'. As it happens, the same tale is told of many churches all over the country - for example, Lincoln Cathedral, where the famous 'Lincoln Imp' is the villain of the tale.

Here is another curious story told by a middle-aged businessman.

> When I was in my late teens I used to hear mumbled conversations and faint voices of people talking to me. My aunt said I was clair-audient, and I should say, 'You are welcome, friend, as long as you don't frighten me'. Anyway, I never said anything and I let it go by.
>
> Twenty years later I was in Walsall trying to find a certain company. I was totally lost, driving round and round. As I came to a set of cross roads for the third time, as plain as day I heard this voice saying to me, 'Turn left, first right and first right again'. My prickles went up. However, I followed the instructions and there, right on front of me, was the company I wanted.

Many folk who believe that they are slightly psychic have remarked how very useful this skill can be. For example, there's a personnel manager of a very successful and well-known company who, when interviewing, uses her skill to assess potential employees.

7. Staffordshire

There have been, throughout the centuries, just a few people who have managed to change the whole course of history. One of these was Alfred the Great. This powerful man and later, his daughter, Ethelfleda, managed to halt the mighty armies of the invading Danes. In 878 he made peace with them, making Watling Street the western boundary so that Staffordshire was saved from Danish rule. Ethelfleda built a line of fortresses from Tamworth in the east to Stafford in the west. Of the Stafford fort, nothing remains but a small piece of walling in Eastgate Street. Staffordshire was very much forgotten for the next six hundred years until, during the sixteenth and seventeenth centuries, the Industrial Revolution brought in workers of all kinds such as miners, ironworkers, potters and glass blowers. They settled primarily in South Staffordshire and the Potteries but the population increased dramatically throughout the county.

The Coffin – Enville

Enville, just beyond the West Midlands boundary, has a new housing estate but Beryl's* house is on the outskirts of the village, surrounded by fields and with a winding country road nearby:

> I have lived in this house for seven years, and I never experienced anything until I came here. There's something not quite right, it's something to do with the house. For the first few years after we moved in, there seemed to be an oppressive power in the living room. Whenever I sat on the settee I felt totally oppressed and fell asleep. Things disappeared. I would put them down in specific places and they would be gone. They were mainly to do with the children – photos, pens, that sort of thing. Very early in the morning I would hear what I thought was the children walking across the landing, I would go to tell them to get back to bed and nobody would be there. I used to go up the stairs at night and you couldn't get up the last two stairs, something would be trying to push you back. I was always ill, with chest infections or something. I have seen blood dripping down our bedroom wall. I had never been interested in psychic things but I began to be aware of something strange here.

My husband has to get to work at 6 am and I come downstairs very early. In our kitchen we have what I call a rubbish area, under the stairs and behind is a curtain where we keep the freezer and everything. I often have this strange feeling when I'm standing near there. Every morning for about a week, I went into the kitchen to make a flask and I felt that there was a shadow behind me.

Then one morning, while the children were playing in another room, I could see the shadow out of the corner of my eye. It was a great black outline and very tall. I telephoned my sister who is very sensitive and told her, 'I have got this awful presence behind me'. She picked it up the other end of the line. She said, 'He's wearing black, he has got a big black hat and he's carrying a stick, the sort of stick they used to have when they walked in front of a funeral cortege. He doesn't like you talking to me and he keeps saying, 'I have come for the children'.' That really frightened me. I said to her, 'How can I get rid of him?' She said, 'I have a friend, Sue, who is a paranormal expert, I will see if Sue can do anything'. I told her, 'I don't like this, I'm going to go now'. My sister said, 'Just be careful, don't stand in the hallway for too long'. With that, the shadow passed through me and the force pushed me hard against the door. It shook me and upset me. By the time Sue arrived it had gone. We lit a few candles but there was no sign of him.

Several weeks later I was talking to a neighbour. I asked him, 'Have you ever had a ghostly happening?' and I told him about my experience. We left the conversation at that but a few days later he saw me and said, 'I have got to tell you this. I was talking to this man I have known for a long time in the village. Fifty years ago his uncle used to drive a bus along the route that went past your house. One day, he was driving past your house when he had to slow down because there was a man was in the middle of the road, walking very slowly and carrying a white child's coffin. He didn't seem to want to move and the driver just kept following him. Then, as the man walked along he slowly disappeared. It upset the driver a bit. He mentioned this to one of the local people who said, 'Don't you know the story? In one of the houses along here a young child died of smallpox. The grandfather wouldn't accept the child's death, and when the child was buried he insisted on carrying the coffin down the road to the burial ground'.

My house was built in the middle of the 1800s and the child died in the 1880's. The village only had a few houses in it then, and my house is quite isolated. It seems to me that this is the house where the grandfather and the family lived. I wonder if my ghost is the grandfather who comes for the children.

David Taylor, of Parasearch, makes an interesting comment:

Research by Dr. Michael Persinger suggests that a large proportion of paranormal activity appears to centre around areas of tectonic stress such as geological faultlines. The work of Persinger and others strongly suggests that in the periods before earthquakes, when naturally occurring geomagnetic fields are at their highest, there is an increase in reports of strange phenomena. In the small South Staffordshire village of Enville there is just such a fault – only a minor one, but maybe one strong enough to help explain some of the strange goings on reported in this beautiful village.

The Spirit Cat – Brownhills

This was a little mining village – or rather a hamlet, as the district of Brownhills was not created until 1877, when five neighbouring places were amalgamated. Many of the inhabitants were miners with a lot of privately-owned mines in the area. A hundred years later a new estate was built in the Clayhanger area and one of the detached houses was bought by Jane and her family:

> We had a spirit cat in our house at Brownhills. It was always on the landing, it used to come out of the bedroom door and trip us up. Both my daughter and I would feel it under our feet and we would hop about, trying to miss it, with the cat dodging about, as they do. I would say, 'It's that blessed cat again!' It would go scuttering through our feet and when we looked down, nothing would be there.
>
> I don't know why it chose our house. We moved in during 1977 when the house was new. My daughter was about 12 and my son was about 13.
>
> Somebody my daughter knew came to the house when he was doing some research on social history. He said, 'I nearly tripped over your ginger cat'. We didn't have a cat, that was our ghost.
>
> We felt it quite regularly, a couple of times a week for a few years then suddenly, for no reason, it just stopped.

There are more ghostly animals in the Worcestershire chapter.

STAFFORDSHIRE ROYAL INFIRMARY

In the 13th century, a hospital opened in Stafford on the eastern side of the town and continued until the 1580s. On that same site, the Staffordshire Royal Infirmary was built, which has now combined with the City General Hospital and the Hartshill Orthopaedic Hospital to become the University Hospital of North Staffordshire, one of the largest hospitals in the UK.

A Tribute

The next two stories were told by Michelle Dalgarno, Shelley to her friends. She was everything that you could want in a nurse. Quite apart from being a beautiful young lady, she was warm-hearted, lively, popular, and efficient. Tragically, she died recently in a road accident.

> In the early 1990s I was living in the old Nurses' home in the Staffordshire Royal Infirmary. About twenty rooms went off this corridor, they had been designed for nurses in training. The room I had was more splendid than the rest, it used to be the old Nursing Sister's room and it had a kitchen and a bathroom. I lived there for about two and a half years. All the time I was there, a woman would appear to me on and off, I used to see her out of the corner of my eye. She would always appear when everybody else was out and I was on my own. I used to sense she was there, I would talk to her, I'd say, 'Morning, how are you today?' If you are on shift work you spend a lot of time on your own and she was company for me. She used to follow me around, it just became second nature. I never thought anything about it.

This went on for a long time. One night, I was sitting on the floor with my friend – I think we were playing cards – when the door banged. We both jumped up and looked at the door at the same time. I looked at my friend and she looked at me and we said to each other, 'Did you see what I saw?' 'What did you see?' 'No, you tell me first'. She had seen a woman, not very tall, in a long cape walk past the open door. I had seen her too, quite clearly, but only down to her feet as she had no feet. I said to my friend that I had felt her presence many times. My friend had lived in the room before me and we both laughed because we couldn't believe that someone else had had the same feelings.

Did we have a ghost in the nurses' home? I asked around. We had a night warden who used to come round and make sure the place was neat and tidy. She brought some old photographs into the office. Apparently, during the war years a bomb had been dropped on the nurses' home and a nurse had been killed. The building had been rebuilt but now it was two feet higher than originally. She had, perhaps, been walking on the old passageway which is two feet lower.

When mum and dad were helping to me to move out, I shouted to my mum and dad to take some things and I ran back to see if there was anybody to whom I could say goodbye. There was nobody in the corridor and nobody in the bathroom. I stood looking out of the window and over the car park behind the nurses home and deaf school, just day-dreaming, wondering what would happen next in my career. Suddenly I felt this presence by the side of me and I clearly heard a middle-aged woman's voice saying, 'You will be alright'. It made me jump. Once again I caught a glimpse of her out of the corner of my eye.

I had felt quite apprehensive about this new phase in my life but after I heard her, I felt quite calm. None of the nurses ever saw her after that, it was as if she left the nurses' home when I did.

The Lost Daughter

This is the second of the Michelle's stories, told before she was so horrifically killed. You can see her sweet, sensitive personality shining through them, and we hope that these will stand as a tribute to her.

I became involved in a very strange story in about 1994, when I was working in the North Staffordshire Royal Infirmary. The Infirmary is in two parts, I was in the old part which used to be a private hospital – now it's been made into an office. It used to be the Acute Admissions Ward and we had some very dramatic cases there. Next door was the old Burns and Plastic Surgery Ward.

We had a lady in her seventies admitted. She was a lovely old lady, very bubbly with sparkling eyes. When she came in she was quite unwell and she was with us for about four days before she went home. In the bed opposite was a young lady who said to me, 'Can I ask you something? – Are there any ghosts in this ward?' I dismissed it a little bit. I laughed and said, 'How many do you want?' She told me that in the middle of the night she had seen a young girl leaning over the old lady and looking at her. She described the young girl very clearly. She said that she had long blond hair tied with yellow ribbons, she wore a yellow dress and was carrying a big bundle. I thought she was a bit odd.

We were having a cup of coffee in the staff room and I was telling the other staff about this when a colleague of mine, a health care assistant, said, 'I have seen her!' She had been working on the ward a couple of nights before, and she had turned round to see a little girl with long blond hair and yellow ribbons coming in carrying a basket. It sounded similar but the one ghost was carrying a bundle and the other a basket. Nothing more came up again.

It must have been about two weeks later when the elderly lady was brought back. I was longing to ask her about the little girl but I didn't know how to put it. How do you say to someone, 'I think you have a ghost?' In the end I said, 'I don't know how to say this but have you lost someone in your family?' She said, 'I lost my daughter, Mary, she was nine when she died'. She asked, 'Why, have you seen her?' I told her that I hadn't, but somebody else had, in fact two people had seen her. I said, 'Could you tell me about your daughter?' She described her as very pretty with long blond hair and I asked her if she ever wore anything special. Her reply was: 'I always liked to dress her in yellow with yellow ribbons and a yellow dress. I had made her a rag doll and she always had this big doll with her.' This is what I presumed the bundle was. She wanted to know who had seen her daughter, and she was obviously quite emotional.

She told me that years ago she and her daughter had decided to go for a picnic at Rudyard Lake. They had a picnic basket and she was putting sandwiches and things in the basket when suddenly it started raining. The mother told her to go and play in her room. Mary went upstairs, then suddenly the mother heard screams. She ran upstairs, the door was shut but she could see bright lights flickering under the door. Her daughter's dress had caught fire. She was rushed to North Staffordshire Infirmary and was in the Burns Ward next door. Just before she died she said, 'I didn't want to tell mummy but I had been playing with the fire. It was my fault that I got burned'. She was in hospital for a long time until she died. The elderly lady then showed me a little cross round her neck. She said, 'I always wear it. We put all her toys in her coffin and I put the cross in there but the vicar took the cross out and said, 'You must always wear it and Mary will stay with you".

Other people had told her that they had seen Mary but I was the first one to tell her she had been seen so clearly. I didn't want to frighten or upset the elderly lady but I thought she would like to know that her daughter was still with her. I felt pleased that I had been a link between the old lady and the two people who had seen her daughter.

David Taylor of Parasearch says:

It is perhaps not surprising that people report ghostly activity in hospitals, to encounter a ghost in a place like this makes far more sense than a churchyard. Such ghostly encounters offer paranormal investigators a dilemma. Assuming that the experience has no logical explanation, then are such reports evidence of the human soul or that emotions and tragic events can be 'recorded' onto the fabric of a building?

Shugborough Hall

The hall is just east of Stafford. The manor of Shugborough originally belonged to the Bishop of Lichfield but in 1642, he sold it to the Anson family. They pulled down the modest manor house and built a three-story house that forms the core of today's mansion. The Anson family prospered and the house grew. In 1747 a descendant became Lord Anson and First Lord of the Admiralty. In 1831 a further descendant was First Earl of Lichfield.

Shugborough Hall is now owned by the National Trust who have converted it to show a complete working historic estate. In the kitchens, the cooks are at work, maids iron the laundry, Victorian gardeners tend the roses. We have a lovely little story from the Hall which came about through a phone-in to Dave Ellis's programme when he was standing in for Ed Doolan:

> My husband was the caretaker at Shugborough Hall and so we moved into the caretaker's flat. We had strange experiences going over a period of four or five years.
>
> My third child, a little girl, was critically ill. I popped out of the room for a minute to fetch something and when I returned, I saw a lady by the bed dressed in Victorian clothing and bending over my daughter. When I entered the room the Victorian lady looked up, put a finger to her mouth as if to say, 'be quiet' and walked away – straight through the wardrobe! This happened several times, until my daughter recovered.
>
> The last time I saw the lady was about a year ago and she was wearing a hat and coat, I assumed she had come to say 'good-bye'.
>
> I was so intrigued that I decided to go down to the archives to see who it might be. A gentleman down there gave me a book to look through and I came across a photo of the lady. She used to be a nanny at Shugborough Hall. From the old photographs she looked just like the ghost I had seen.
>
> The family always said it was my daughter's guardian angel.

Are You Alright Duck? – Barlaston

Barlaston is about ten miles north of Stafford and near to the Wedgwood Visitor's Centre. Bartonland is a thirteen-bedroomed house built in the early 1800s for the Johnson family who owned most of the Potteries. When it closed in April 1992 it had been a home for the elderly for some years. One of the staff, Val, told us:

We used to notice inexplicable noises coming from the third floor when no-one was there, a curious rustling and rattling. Small items would go missing then reappear in places where they could not possibly have been, and furniture was often moved round during the night. One room was left empty for a couple of weeks and during this time the alarm bell there ran over and over again. Another time, two of the staff were tidying a locker when fruit from a bowl on top of it suddenly flew of in all directions. The staff screamed and ran out of the room.

No-one living or working in the home smoked, yet sometimes we could smell cigarette smoke, so we decided that if we did have a ghost, it must be male, and we called him Charlie. When something weird happened we would say to each other, 'Charlie's at it again'.

Bartonland closed and the residents were transferred to other homes. When the last resident had gone, the staff decided that one of them had better stay each night to guard the premises. Neil, the gardener, said he would take first turn. He was a big strapping fellow, six feet tall and ready to tackle anything.

When we arrived the morning after his all-night vigil, he was sitting in the front porch with his Alsatian dog. He said that nothing would persuade him to go inside the house again. He was so serious and so scared that we all had to believe his story. He said that while he was sitting in the lounge, watching the T.V., a horrible feeling came over him. The dog growled and its hairs all stood on end. Then he clearly heard an elderly woman's voice saying, in a Potteries accent, 'Are you alright duck?' His dog flew out of the room and he followed.

To think that we had been calling the ghost 'Charlie' when it was female. Or did we have two ghosts?

Ghosts seem to be very unstable and repeatedly change sex, mode of dress or metamorphose into completely different apparitions. The traditional ghost at Wick with a red dress has more recently been seen in blue. Or, are these different ghosts? Haunted houses often claim more than one ghost. In *Midland Ghosts and Hauntings*, a mother who lives in Stratford-upon-Avon claims to have a dozen different ghosts in her house. She says, 'Most people don't seem to realise that ghosts don't take up any space so you can have a dozen, say, living quite happily in one house'.

8. Warwickshire

With its fertile farmland and plentiful water supply, Warwickshire has been occupied and fought over for thousands of years. All this has resulted in a county full of folklore, legends and ghosts, both traditional and modern.

For centuries it was dominated by great forests, the Forest of Arden covered most of the county northwest of the Avon. Within these dark forests conspirators gathered and plots were hatched. For centuries, Warwickshire was a thorn in the side of the monarchy. In 1312, Piers Gaveston, the king's favourite, was kidnapped by the Earl of Warwick and beheaded without trial on Blacklow Hill. Many Warwickshire labourers joined the Peasant's Rising under Wat Tyler in 1381. Warwickshire played a significant part in the War of the Roses - Coventry was a stronghold of the House of Lancaster while Warwick supported the House of York. Many aristocratic families in Warwickshire refused to acknowledge Henry VIII as the supreme head of the Church, and were frequently plotting to put a Roman Catholic on the throne. On 5th November 1605 about a hundred sympathisers gathered on Dunsmore Heath, ready to whisk away the young Queen Elizabeth, daughter of James I, if the gunpowder plot succeeded. In 1642, the opening stages of the civil war took place in Warwickshire.

The crowning glory of Warwick is, of course, Warwick Castle, standing on a precipitous cliff between the town and the Avon. It dates back to the time of the Danish invasions and was begun by Ethelfleda in about 915, but has been developed time and time again into a stately Palace, visited frequently by Royalty. The castle was home to the Earls of Warwick until 1978 when it was bought by the Tussauds group. The haunted tower at Warwick Castle is occupied by Sir Fulke Greville. It is said that he spent so much money on the castle he had little left for his staff. When, in 1628, his manservant, Ralph Haywood, heard how little he was getting from his master's will, he drew a knife and stabbed Sir Fulke. Realising the enormity of his actions, he turned the knife on himself. Sir Fulke took 27 days to die.

A lesser-known ghost is that of Sir Fulke's grandfather, also Fulke Greville, who is buried in Alcester Church. Bellringers hear phantom footsteps, a previous verger complained about something brushing past him at night and a lady polishing the church plate turned round to find Sir Fulke standing behind her. She promptly fainted.

Fulford Hall – Earlswood

Earlswood is famous for its huge attractive lakes, which are actually three man-made reservoirs known as Engine Pool, Windmill Pool and Terry's Pool. They were created in the 1820s to feed the Stratford-upon-Avon canal.

About a kilometre to the northwest of Earlswood Lakes is the rambling old mansion of Fulford Hall, about which are many strange rumours. The house was built in about 1897 by Colonel Johnson on land bought from the railway company. Half a century ago it hosted huge music festivals with scenes of skirmishes and orgies, then it lay derelict and empty for years. The sons of a local farmer rode their motor bikes up and down the stairs. Hippies moved in and local builders stole chunks of carving. When John Yorke bought the house and began its restoration, rumour has it that he saw a ghost in the garden.

The house has now been fully restored and has kicked off the traces of its unusual past, except for a number of inexplicable accidents near its entrance gates. Cars, when rounding the bed, shoot across the road for no reason. A local resident says, 'Only a few weeks ago we had police sirens and helicopters because a young girl was injured. She had no idea why her car went out of control'. Another person who once found himself going through the hedge is a retired teacher, now choir master. Some 30 years ago he was Leader of a local scout group and he says:

> The owner of Fulford Hall let us camp in his fields. As my daughter had just been born, I didn't stay there overnight but went home in the evening, leaving the scouts in the care of other staff.
>
> I left the field one evening and began driving home in the twilight, but I had only gone a short way when, for no reason at all, the car suddenly went out of control, shot through a hedge and into a field.
>
> I was sitting there quite dazed and wondering what had happened when some youngsters came and tapped at the window. I wound the window down and they said, 'We will push you out back on to the road again'. I asked them how they knew that I was there. They said, 'You aren't the first, you're the third one tonight. This is JJ's night. There's a stone here in the grass verge and if you look at it you will see that it's the same date'. Sure enough, there it was, engraved June 15th, 1895.

When I returned the next morning I looked at the hedge and saw that where I had gone through the hedge there wasn't a mark on the hedge and there wasn't a mark on the car. I don't believe in ghosts or any of this psychic nonsense but you explain that.

The owner of Fulford Hall sometimes came to visit us and one evening he told the following story:

"Jack Johnson was the owner of Fulford Hall in the late nineteenth century and tradition has it that he was a miserly, miserable man. One night he was riding round the perimeter of the estate, looking for poachers, when he saw two men who were after his rabbits. Some of the village folk were so poor that's all they had to live on – rabbits.

'Although JJ was plagued with rabbits, he was furious that someone should try to steal them. He stood in his stirrups and rode straight at the first poacher, knocking him down and riding the horse straight over him. Still standing in his stirrups, he levelled his blunderbuss, aiming at the second poacher. In those days the road had not been metalled and was just a path, and he evidently forgot that there was a tree right next to the road with a low branch across it. Furthermore, he was riding against the light. Suddenly there was a crash and his teeth bit the branch. This had the unfortunate result that it took his head off. The head stayed in the tree while he slithered out of the saddle on to the floor. The head then fell out of the tree on top of the body. Four or five years later a stone was erected on that very spot.

'Once a year, on the anniversary of his death, JJ comes riding at night round the periphery of his estate. You can hear the clippetty-clop of his horses hooves, but when he reaches the spot where the tree once stood, the noise stops, then you hear a crash followed by a soft thud as his head drops out of the tree."

The stone is still there, near the entrance gates of Fulford Hall. It stands over half a metre in height and has a rounded top. The engravings read simply, JJ June 15 1895.

The moral of this story is that if you are driving along the road from Earlswood Station to Tidbury Green, take care, especially if it's night-time and especially if the date is 15th June.

The Invisible Motorist – Arrow

The tiny rural village of Arrow is near to Ragley Hall and most of the residents were once workers at the hall. The entrance and exit gates are a mile apart and about halfway between these two gates is a spring and a little stile set in the hedge, known as 'The Springs'. Towards the end of the 19th century passing vehicles - coaches, horses and carts and so on, would be flagged down by a little old lady who asked for a lift to Dunnington Cross Roads. However, when the driver stopped to set her down, she had disappeared. This became such a nuisance that a deputation visited the Marquise and asked if something could be done about it. The site round the spring was excavated and the bones of a little old lady found. She was re-interred in consecrated ground. The phantom hitch-hiker disappeared but the White Lady of the Springs has frequently appeared to passersby.

This is an ancient settlement. There was a stately home on the site of Ragley Hall in the 6th century, and Arrow Church, St. James, has parts going back to the 1200s. Jane* regularly attends a church meeting there which is on a Friday night from 7.30 to 9.00 pm. She says:

> I was driving when I left the church with a friend in October 2004. We got to the entrance of the church and the car stalled. As far as I can remember, it has never stalled before. Seconds later a car sped past the entrance at a great speed, if my car hadn't stalled I would have gone into the side of it. Opposite the church is a quiet road, when I started to go down it I felt as if an invisible presence took the steering wheel out of my hands and the car swerved right across the road. We were terrified so we started saying the Lord's prayer out loud. Seconds later, I felt as if the presence was leaving the car and I found that I was in control again.
>
> Another incident occurred in the same month. We left the same church at about 9.20 in the evening and this time, my friend was driving. Sometimes, she liked to have a drive round before going home and so we went a long way round. As we were driving through Cookhill we saw the shape of a person bending over in the road. We both said, 'What's that?' It looked as if it had a cape on, but we couldn't see any details. As we got closer it disappeared.

The Cock and the Treasure – Near Stratford

The old Roman road, the A422, from Stratford to Redditch is a long, lonely road, passing through lush farmland. For centuries it was the haunt of highway robbers and other evil characters. About six miles out of Stratford are cross roads leading to Haselor on the right and Temple Grafton on the left. Just past here, on the left, near to where the bypass begins, in a piece of woodland, is a conical hill, known locally as 'Alcock's Arbour'. An 'arbour' is usually a shaded walk or a bench surrounded by trees.

The Alcock's were an influential family in Stratford-upon-Avon. In the mid 1500s Edward Alcock, was subcosts of the Stratford Guilds and Colleges and a most unpopular character. During his time he removed all the images in local churches under the guise of Protestantism.

In the 1600s, Sir William Dugdale, wrote that the hill was 'by the common people called Alcock's Arbour, towards the foot whereof is a hole, now almost filled up, having been the entrance into a cave, as the inhabitants report of which cave there is an old wives story that passes for current amongst people of the adjacent towns, viz, that one Alcock, a great robber, used to lodge therein and having got much money by that course of life, hid it in an iron-bound chest whereunto were 3 keys, which chest they say is still there, but guarded by a cock that continually sits upon it'. Dugdale goes on to say that a long time ago, an Oxford scholar found the chest and managed to open two of the locks, but as he tried to open the third, the cockerel seized him and tore him to pieces. According to the legend, if you find one of Alcock's bones and show it to the bird, it will let you open the treasure. Another old tale says that a local farmer tried to pull the chest out of the cave. He threw some ropes round the chest and attached them to the harness of his horses but the chest was too heavy to move.

During the general chat after a meeting in Stratford-upon-Avon in about 2003, Maisie* said that on the hill was a farm, also known as Alcock's Arbour, and:

> My cousins and aunts lived there for a short time. When they explored the cellars, they found all sorts of strange things, old purses, old costume jewellery, rotted parasols, old clothes and so on. It was said that highwaymen used to ride up and down this road, stopping the coaches. One of the highwaymen must have lived at the house and he must have taken some people into the house and locked them in the cellar because of the artefacts that were found.
>
> One lunch time, some builders were sitting at the bottom of the stairs, eating their bread and cheese with their dog lying across the stairs, when suddenly his hackles rose and he began to howl. They looked up the stairs and there was a lady in an old-fashioned dress. At first, they thought it was one of the workmates all dressed up, but it wasn't. From that time onwards the dog would never go in the house. The atmosphere of the house was not very pleasant and nobody stayed there for long. The farm was pulled down after the Second World War.

Now for the interesting bit. When the new road to Evesham was built, excavations took place in the area which were of such importance that television's 'Time Team' was involved. They discovered that the mound was, in fact, the tomb of a Celtic chief. A little room would have been made for him containing day-to-day artefacts and his precious possessions. Then the whole would have been buried under the enormous mound, now the hill.

No doubt some earth fell away to make access to the burial chamber and the precious artefacts. Perhaps an Oxford scholar understood through his studies that it was the site of a burial mound and came to find the treasure, although that doesn't explain his three keys. And where does the cock come in? Perhaps a cockerel adopted the cave. Or the medievals were into symbolism in a big way, cocks could represent vigilance and courage in battle but they were also thought to have strange powers and warned of danger. Perhaps the cock and the three locks were medieval embellishments to the discovery of the tomb.

Perhaps Edward Alcock, when he removed the treasures from the churches, kept some of them in a chest bound by three locks.

What are we to make of the robbers at the cave and at Alcock's Arbour? This is anybody's guess. Perhaps a descendant of Alcock's gambled away the family fortune and turned to highway robbery, as the young bloods did in the 1700s. It would be interesting to have a more detailed list of the finds, if Maisie reads this story please could she get in touch with Hunt End Books, 01527 542516.

The Blue Vase – Wootton Wawen

Wootton Wawen has Saxon roots and claims to be the oldest village in Warwickshire. The name comes from 'wudu' meaning wood and tun, an enclosed piece of land. Wagen held the land before the Norman's arrived in 1066. Parts of the church, St. Peter's, are Anglo-Saxon.

A previous caretaker always declared that the church was haunted. She would see lights in the church when she was certain that she had switched them all off. Before leaving, she would close the piano lid and put away the music book but in the morning when she returned, the piano would be open and the book would be placed on the piano stand.

In medieval times an old priory stood next to the church but it has now completely disappeared. During the time of the plague, Coventry ran out of places in which to bury their dead so a large plague pit was dug in St. Peter's Churchyard and the plague victims buried there. It's still there, known as The Coventry Piece and is where the ashes are scattered. Ever since that time two ghostly monks have walked along the side of the church to kneel and pray at the Coventry Piece. They were last seen about fifteen years ago by a caretaker.

Only a few yards from the church is the magnificent Wootton Wawen Hall, the favourite haunt of the Prince of Wales (later George IV). It was here that his romance with the widow Maria Ann Fitzherbert blossomed and flourished. At first, she would have nothing to do with him but he stabbed himself in the arm to get her attention. Although he had various mistresses and was later morganatically married to Caroline of Brunswick, partly to settle his debts, Maria was always his great love and remained his favourite paramour to the end of his days. Now she manifests herself in the house by a beautiful perfume. At a banker's conference, the delegates asked what the wonderful perfume was, and the owner of the house replied, 'That's our Mrs. Fitz'.

Part of the site is occupied by residential caravans and Lucy* lived in one in the 1970s. She says:

> Wootton Wawen is well-known for the perfume of Lady Fitzherbert which blows through the whole estate. The residential caravans on the estate are now mostly occupied by elderly people but when I lived in one there was quite a community of young people living there. They had all experienced the odour of Lady Fitzherbert.
>
> A lot of people saw the grey lady, which is a different manifestation to that of Lady Fitzherbert and is thought to be an old housekeeper. One cold and

frosty evening I sat up late in the Country Club, which is on the estate, watching T.V. A middle-aged man, George, came in and he was shaking. He said, 'I've just seen the grey lady. I was walking over the bridge when the dog started to growl, I looked up to see what the dog was staring at and there was the grey lady looking down at me'. He added that he could see the figure perfectly clearly. She was wearing a cloak with a hood, but there was no face, he could see the red lining inside the hood.

A little girl lived in a flat at the hall and she regularly used to chatter away. It wasn't until she grew older and learned to speak properly that her parents realised she was having conversations with a mysterious lady.

In the foyer of the main hall was a blue vase with the remnants of Lord Carrington's heart. He was the 17th century owner of the hall, his grandfather had married a Throckmorton, consequently he was a Roman Catholic and because of the religious persecutions of the time he had to live on the continent. There he was murdered by his manservant for his horse and his money. His heart was returned to Wootton Wawen and the story goes that since that time the house has been haunted. A friend of ours, Pauline, used to clean the hall and she regularly had dealings with a playful spirit. It would pinch her backside and keep moving things – it would move a chair to one side to block her path. She would be cleaning and the vacuum would go off, she would say, 'Fred, put it on again' and you would see the switch go down and the vacuum would start to work again. Most mornings, when she arrived, all the pictures had been turned with their faces towards the wall. Pauline told us that if she moved the vase, the next morning she would always find it back in the proper alcove, even when there was no-one in the house.

In the estate grounds is 'The Country Club', a club for caravan dwellers. There's a cellar downstairs, it's reputed to have several tunnels off it leading to the hall and the local church although they are now bricked up. Cliff, who was then the licensee, asked a couple of lads, Roger and John, to go into the cellar to change a barrel. They tootled off down the steps into the cellar but twenty minutes later they hadn't reappeared. We said, 'Where are they?' and we went to have a look for them. Just as we got to the cellar steps we saw them coming back up with their eyes wide open. They had seen two monks walk across the bottom of the steps and into the wall on the other side.

Phantom Footsteps – Welford-on-Avon

The pretty village of Welford with its thatched houses is more than 1,400 years old having been established in Saxon times. The caravan sites on the Avon are popular with holiday-makers from local towns as the husbands can go fishing and the wives can go shopping in nearby Stratford.

A pub by the river is known as the 'Four Alls' because of the four stained glass portraits in the bar, of a soldier, a priest, a king and a yeoman. The soldier has the inscription, 'Fight All', the priest, 'Pray All', the king 'Rule All' and the yeoman 'Pay All'.

The next piece was told at the Evesham Arts Centre in 2005:

> My aunt, Win Basson, lived in an old three-storey house in Welford-on-Avon. Most nights they would hear these footsteps coming up the stairs, then they would be aware of the bedroom door being opened. Something would come into the bedroom and walk round her bed tucking her in as it went. It would then go to the wardrobe door, open and close it, go the bedroom door, open it and walk out, then close it. I don't think they ever saw anything, just heard it.

STRATFORD-ON-AVON

In 1196 the bishop of Worcester laid out a new town, covering 109 acres, on the edge of an existing Saxon village beside an ancient crossing of the river Avon. Six streets were planned, three parallel to the river and three at right angles to it. This basic plan lies unchanged at the heart of Stratford-upon-Avon today.

By Shakespeare's time, Stratford was still a small and leafy town of about 200 houses, with many orchards, gardens and trees. Shakespeare's father was a prominent man in the town, rising to the position of bailiff. William went to London where he prospered as a playwright and, in 1613, his life's work complete, he retired to Stratford.

The following tale is one of the many hauntings in this ancient town. In *Strange Meetings* a little girl sees an angel the night before her uncle dies in the room next door and there's also the story of a lady who comes out of a cupboard in the evenings for a chat. One family had a male ghost called Fred which they contemplating mating with their friend's female ghost known as Miranda.

Immortalised

The Royal Shakespeare Theatre was completed in 1932. An earlier theatre, opened on Shakespeare's birthday in 1879, was destroyed by fire in 1926.

Josh Dale told this story in 2002 when he was only thirteen but already a seasoned performer. In the summer of 2001 he was selected to take part in 'The Prisoners Dilemma', a new play by David Edgar, performed by the Royal Shakespeare Company at The Other Place.

As Josh is under age, he has to have a chaperone to look after him, even during rehearsals. She looks after his general welfare, fetching him food and drink and keeping him occupied during his stage appearances, usually by playing Scrabble. The chaperone also acts as a link between the actor and the director. Josh says:

Ann was usually my chaperone, we built up quite a relationship and got on like a house on fire. Occasionally it was Bridget. When Bridget and I were alone backstage one evening we heard someone going up and down some steps at the back of the stage, then a knocking at the door. We opened the door to see who it was and no-one was there.

One evening, during the last scene, I was hanging about in the wings waiting to go on stage and I found that I was on my own. There's a quick change on stage and everybody was busy. It's strange being there on your own, I felt nervous even though there were people on the stage. I found myself thinking sad, pessimistic thoughts, such as 'What if I forget my lines?'

There's a high part behind the stage, about one and a half times the height of a room, where they were going to put a band (there's a live band) but they decided not to. Part of it sticks out and there's railings along it. I didn't have anything to do, so I was looking round and happened to glance up and there, by the railings, was this grey-white glow. I couldn't see any particular details but the glow was in the shape of a person, just standing there.

I didn't think too much about it until my mother told me that a woman had hung herself there. All round the walls are pictures of past actresses and other characters who helped in the theatre and among them is a portrait of the woman who committed suicide.

Theatre staff confirmed that an actress had committed suicide there but did not want her to be named.

The Sleepwalker

The house is the next story is very near to the centre of the town and the story comes from the occupant:

This house was built in 1957 to a married couple's specifications. They raised their children here and lived in the house until they died. You can feel that it's a happy house, with a nice atmosphere.

We have a seven-year old daughter and outside her bedroom, on the landing, is a pendant with three lights. These light bulbs keep popping. It is just ridiculous. We have used at least 30 in the last few weeks. It doesn't happen anywhere else in the house and we have called in the electrician who says that there is no electrical problem.

Just before I went to bed one night I went in to check on my daughter and saw that she was fast asleep. I got into my bed, turned the light off and I heard her get out of bed and go across the landing. I distinctly heard the pattering of small feet. I waited for the noise of the pull cord in the bathroom and for the sound of her feet returning to her bedroom but nothing happened. I got out of bed and went to the landing, expecting her to be there, but she wasn't. I went into her bedroom and she was still there, fast asleep, in the same position that

I had seen her earlier. We have a very sensitive burglar alarm and nothing was picked up.

Something turned the heating on. As my husband went up to bed he realised that the heating was on when we had definitely switched it off. Because of this, he decided to double-check the following evening and it had been turned on again. My mother had been staying with us so I 'phoned her but she said she hadn't switched it on. In any case, she wouldn't know how to do it, she's scared of things like that. It's just as if somebody is playing practical jokes.

Sometimes my husband calls, 'What do you want?' and I haven't said anything. Occasionally I have been sitting at my dressing table with the bedroom door open so that I can see on to the landing and out of the corner of my eye I can see somebody coming up the stairs but when I turn and look no-one is there.

I'm very sceptical about ghosts and I tend to think that it's something to do with my daughter, giving out some kind of energy. She sleepwalks and she talks in her sleep.

A wise thought. This kind of paranormal activity tends to be centred round a certain person, usually female and in most cases, a young teenager, but in this case, the daughter is only seven years old.

The Man-hating Ghost

Near the centre of Stratford is a large and flourishing hotel with a secret. The receptionist must never put a single man in one of its rooms. She can put married couples in and families but there's trouble whenever a single man is put in there. Susan* once worked at the hotel and says:

A man came in very late one night and was desperate for a room. The receptionist looked on the computer and she could see that all the rooms were booked except for this certain room. As she was sceptical about the rumour anyway, she put the man in there.

Early the next morning the man came running down to the reception desk in his underpants. He said that he was sleeping face down in bed when something came into the room and sat on his back and began clawing him. It had pinned him face down on the bed. When the receptionist looked at his back, he had scratch marks all down his back.

The hotel is a converted house. The story goes that the owner was very cruel to his wife and daughter, and often locked them in the cupboard in that room. Now the wife haunts the room and likes to get her own back on any single man who sleeps in there.

It's very unusual for anyone to be hurt by a ghost. They're usually quite harmless creatures, in fact some people are very fond of their ghosts. There's a lady in Bromsgrove whose husband is away a great deal and in the evenings she gets out her knitting and is joined by a lavender lady. She says she enjoys the company.

Something came into the room and sat on his back and began clawing him… he had scratch marks all down his back.

Frozen with Fear

No-one has any idea why the twelve-year old in the next story should see a Victorian lady in his bedroom. He lives in a new house built on farmland:

> When I was twelve, I saw a Victorian lady in our house. She came into my bedroom. I was really scared, I was sweating and shaking and frozen with fear.
>
> It usually takes me about an hour to go to sleep. I had closed my eyes and was trying to go to sleep but I wasn't tired. Suddenly, I felt the temperature of the room change and it became cold. I opened my eyes and there she was. She was thin, in her twenties and dressed in white. I got the feeling she was wearing a satin dress with a little floral pattern on it, part of it was a dark satin and part of it was light. I think it was a kind of pink. She had fairly long hair, quite dark. To start with, her mood was absolutely fine and she was just wandering round my bedroom. Then all of a sudden she had a total mood swing. She started stamping around. She went over to my wardrobe unit and shook the whole unit. That really scared me. After a few minutes her mood returned to normal and she disappeared. I ran into my parents' room and slept there for the night.
>
> I know I wasn't asleep – although I closed my eyes I didn't fall asleep and when she disappeared I didn't wake up in order to run into my parents' room.

Who's Been Living in My House? – Tiddington

The next story-teller lived in an old cottage in Tiddington, a small village just south of Stratford.

> Each night, there was a creaking of doors that you could never explain and we would get up each morning to find that doors, that we knew we had closed before we went to bed, were open.
>
> I knew the lady who lived in the house before us, she was an elderly spinster, well into her nineties. Six months after we moved in, my wife told me that she had seen an elderly lady in the room. From her description, it sounded very much like the spinster. My daughter, who was only five, knew her well and one morning she said, 'Oh, Miss B... came into my room last night'.
>
> Of course, we never said a thing about this to the people who bought the house after us, but they told us that both the lady of the house and her daughter had seen an elderly lady in there.

On the whole, if someone moves into a house which has the reputation of being haunted, they have no problems. To see a ghost you usually need to have a particular kind of sensitivity and it's unlikely that two successive house owners should both have that sensitivity.

The Resident Ghost – Charlecote Park (National Trust)

The Lucy family has held the manor of Charlecote for more than 800 years. The house was begun by Sir Thomas Lucy in 1558 so that part is Elizabethan but it was built chiefly in the 1800s. In 1892 the manor descended to a female Lucy who married a Fairfax so the name was changed to Fairfax-Lucy. It was handed over to the National Trust in 1946.

Sir Thomas Lucy was immortalised by Shakespeare, who poked fun at him by portraying him as Justice Shallow in Henry IV Part 2 and the Merry Wives of Windsor. Sir Thomas was a magistrate and Shakespeare had come before him charged with poaching the magistrate's deer. Shakespeare may have been whipped or sent to prison for a short time. It is said that the Lucy family were so annoyed by the caricature that the relevant pages were torn out of all the copies in their library.

Jessie Love's daughter gives us this lovely picture of a team of young ladies visiting stately homes including Charlecote Park:

> My mother was Jessie Love and she lived in Stratford several years before the First World War. There are still members of the Love family living in Stratford. She was a young girl working in a team of ladies going round stately homes doing repairs. They would stay several days in each house.
>
> The team went to Charlecote Park where my mother was working on the draperies and curtains. In the house is a long staircase and a balcony, the girls were sleeping in a room on the left. After a few days they got to know all the staff except one, a lady in a long black dress who, early every morning, walked along the balcony and into the mistresses' room. They didn't see her during the rest of the day. They mentioned this to the woman who looked after the house and she said, 'Oh you have seen our resident ghost!'

Who Seeks Sir Guy? – Guy's Cliff

The area containing Guy's Cliff and Blacklow Hill was one of the most beautiful and historic parts of Warwickshire before it was ruined by running two fast roads, the A429 and the A46 right through it. West of the A46 is Gaveston's Cross, by Blacklow Hill, where Guy of Warwick, (nicknamed 'The Black Dog of Arden) had the king's favourite, Piers Gaveston, beheaded in 1312. Guy of Warwick had to seek sanctuary in Bordesley Abbey, in Redditch which he now haunts in the form of a black dog. East of the A429 and beyond Saxon Mill are the spectacular heights of Guy's Cliff. They soar above the river Avon and are topped by the ruins of a mansion built in the late 18th century.

At the foot of Guy's Cliff is a large cave, linked with a romantic ballad from the 12th century. In medieval times, the tourists flocked to Guy's Cliff in the same way that they visit Stratford today. Guy was the son of a Northumbrian nobleman who had fallen on hard times. He worked for the Earl of Warwick and fell in love with Felice, the Earl's daughter. He asked for her hand in marriage but Felice said that he must first prove his worth as her husband. After a number of hair-raising adventures he returned to Felice, who again rejected him. After more adventures, which included killing the Dun Cow, a wild boar and a dragon, he returned to Felice who now accepted him as her husband. However, married life did not suit him and he was soon off again to more adventures. When he returned many years later he was so old and battle-scarred that he chose not to return to his wife but to live near her in the cave at Guy's Cliff. When he was dying, he sent to her a ring (or in some versions, a half ring) that proved his identity. Felice rushed to him but he died in her arms. Unable to face life without him (although she had spent most of her life alone) Felice leapt to her death from the cave into the river below.

Now, say the locals, from time to time on foggy evenings a dark funeral cortege has been seen winding its way along the bed of the river. There are other ghost stories, for example, in *Midland Ghosts and Hauntings* a lady who lives nearby woke up to find a character dressed like Piers Gaveston standing by her bed.

About 20 years ago a young family moved to Warwick. The mother says:

> I enrolled my daughter in the riding school belonging to the person who lived at the front of Guys Cliff. Between the chapel and the house was a narrow path and when my children were out riding I used to amuse myself by exploring. One day, I thought I would take a walk along Guy's Cliff to find the cave where Guy is said to have lived as a hermit. It's fenced off with a chain but it's easy to step over the chain. As I was walking along this narrow path, I noticed in front of me a woman, who also seemed to be exploring the path. Her dress was very unusual, it wasn't white and on reflection it was probably medieval. Suddenly, she wasn't there, and there wasn't anywhere she could have gone.

ROYAL LEAMINGTON SPA

The town was planned as a grid with the Parade as its main street, intersected at right angles by Regent Street and Warwick Street. The early name was Leamington Priors, due to its association with the priory at Kenilworth, but in 1838 it was named Royal Leamington Spa by permission of Queen Victoria, who had just visited the town. Leamington's saline springs had been known for centuries but were not developed commercially until the early 1800s. Dr. Henry Jephson, a popular physician, set up practice in the town in 1828 and attracted many blue-blooded patients, including Queen Victoria, so that it became a fashionable resort. He is remembered by the Jephson gardens. Leamington still has an up-market ambience with a range of exclusive shops.

Terror at the Hotel

Near the centre of the town is a large early Victorian hotel. Kerry, a fire alarm engineer, was called out one night to a 'fault' on the fire alarm.

The House originally belonged to the local squire, and the story goes that he got one of the serving girls pregnant, and locked her in a room and starved her to death. This room is now part of the hotel, and various reports of odd happenings have occurred over the years. The wing in which the room is located is closed during the winter as there are insufficient guests to keep it open. Two members of staff make a security patrol at intervals to check on the wing.

During one of the patrols, the fire escape door at the end of the corridor where the haunted room was located was open. The staff members on patrol immediately rang the police who came with tracker dogs. The door was opened from the inside, but there were no footprints in the snow outside, and the dogs found no scent. The police secured the area, and left.

On the next patrol, the same thing happened, and police were called again. Again there were no tracks or scents found. On the 3rd patrol, the door to the haunted room was open, and the lights on. The male member of staff charged into the room to confront the intruder. The door slammed behind him, and the lights and T.V. started to flash on and off.

The female member of staff couldn't open the door from the outside, but strangely couldn't hear any noise from inside. The male member of staff inside was screaming so loudly, the other members of staff in the staff quarters, which was some distance away heard him, and came running armed with kitchen knives and cricket bats.

As they ran into the corridor, the door to the haunted room burst open, and the male member of staff charged out in utter terror. They all ran down the stairs into the reception. The hotel used a pager system so that if the staff were on patrol, and a guest rang for room service, the pager would operate and display the room number. As they ran down the stairs the pager operated and displayed the number of the haunted room...

They locked themselves in the staff quarters, and abandoned the hotel until morning. During this time the fire alarm operated for no reason. I was called in to investigate the fire alarm, and the staff took a lot of persuasion to tell me the story. They were very agitated, and were frightened of having to make a report to head office explaining why they had called the police twice and abandoned the hotel.

If you own a business and if you have any poltergeist activity, the recommended course of action is to have a quiet chat to the staff and find out if anyone has previously experienced anything similar. If you find someone, this is probably the person around which it is centred. However, sometimes one person can act as a catalyst to another person when neither of them have had any problems previously. Don't forget that poltergeists are attracted by people who are ill, miserable or under stress. Make sure that all your employees are healthy and happy in their work!

The Guardian Angel

Mary* has been living in the same house in Leamington Spa now for almost nine years. She says:

> Almost from the first day that I moved in here I felt that someone was watching me, but I thought it was just my imagination and I tried to ignore it. I have this feeling every night.
>
> Lots of strange things happen. Doors slowly open and close and the light will go dim. Sometimes my alarm goes off at 5 o'clock in the morning for no reason. Sometimes the clock is turned forwards or backwards. We have a musty smell or a lavender smell. Often people 'phone me and it sounds as if the phone is ringing their end but it doesn't ring here. The speaker on the Answerphone doesn't come on and the tape recorder doesn't take the message, there's just a long crackle. Things fall off the unit for no reason. I sometimes hear the clattering of dishes in the kitchen, my sister has heard it too. I have a portable telly in my bedroom and that turns itself on. Twice I have been fast asleep in bed and I have been woken up as I felt myself dragged over the bed to the other side (I have a double bed). I now leave the light on until about 2.30 am.
>
> Things are moved round or go missing, then they turn up a week later in the place where they were supposed to be. One day me and my mum were cleaning the unit when I asked her to get a vase from behind a mirror. She said, 'I can't see a vase'. We couldn't find it and I had definitely put it there the day before. Two weeks later there was the vase, behind the mirror. I phoned my mum and said 'I've found the vase'. She asked where it was and when I told her it was behind the mirror she remarked, 'It can't be'.
>
> One day one of my friends was staying in the house. She put her makeup bag on the chair and propped it upright. We heard a rustle and when we looked a couple of make-up things had jumped out of her bag and were lying on the chair.
>
> During the first few years I kept seeing a shadow walk down the hallway. You can just make out that the shadow is a person then you blink and it has gone. It's only there for a second or two. I used to go down and see who it was. Again, I thought it was my imagination. Then one day, when my next door neighbour was visiting me, I saw this shadow going through the doorway. I said to him, 'You must have seen that shadow'. He said, 'Well, I did, I think you have got the same as we have, it's a ghost'. He sometimes had a woman coming into his house in an old-fashioned bride's dress.

I started to think, 'I have a ghost here'. I said to my mum that I thought I had a ghost and she said 'I know'. Evidently she came here one day when I was at work to do a bit of my housework for a treat. She went into the bathroom and someone was in there – she saw a woman in her late thirties or early forties. She said, 'Excuse me' and closed the door. When she looked in a few minutes later nobody was there and no-one had come out.

Early one morning I was asleep in bed when I heard a woman's voice. It said, 'Mary, it's time to get up now'. No-one else was in the house. One cold night I was lying in bed when I felt someone tucking me in, pushing the duvet under the mattress.

Me and my sister were watching 'Birds of a Feather' when they had a Ouija board out on the programme. A shadow walked through the telly very slowly and disappeared. You could tell it was an adult. It hasn't done that before, usually it's gone after a second or two.

I have a budgie which talks to you and sometimes it talks to one of the doors. I have another budgie which will chat for half an hour to someone. Neither of them seem frightened.

My friend was looking in the mirror in the hallway when she suddenly shuddered. I asked her, 'What's the matter'. She said, 'Something has just run over my grave'. I told the ghost not to do that again to my friend and it hasn't happened again.

One day, there was a musty smell and I saw a ball of haze. I said, 'If you are going to show yourself, I don't want to see you. It will frighten me and I will get help to move you on'. I have said to the ghost, 'If at any time you are unhappy and you want to move on just appear and I will arrange it'.

I know when she's around because it goes very cold. You just stand there and you have a shiver down your spine and your hair stands on end. It doesn't bother me, I just tell her to go away. When I'm speaking to one of my friends, she can feel the cold down the phone.

Now and again you can hear the ghost crying. My younger sister says that the ghost comes to sit on the bottom of her bed and cries. Once she asked my sister, 'What are you doing here?' My sister said, 'Oh do go away'.

I don't tell my nephews that there is a ghost in here but one of them, when he was only about six or seven, came running out of the bedroom and asked, 'Who died here before?' I told him, 'Nobody, it's a new building'. He said, 'Somebody has been here before'. My other nephew asked, 'Which lady died in here?' I asked him, 'What can you see?', but he wouldn't tell me, he said, 'Oh nothing'. He wouldn't sleep in that bedroom. He said, 'I want to sleep with you'.

My dad says it's my guardian angel. Three and a half years ago I had a bad car accident. On that morning, my keys were missing and it took me several minutes to find them. I think she meant that as a warning. A car crashed into mine and I was pushed sideways. The ambulance men said that I should have died in the accident. When I 'phoned my older sister to tell her that I had been in a car accident, she said that she had dreamed that a white car hit me and knocked me over to the other side of the road, which is what happened. I said to her, 'Why didn't you tell me and then I could have watched out for it?' She answered, 'I didn't know it was going to come true, it was just a dream'. She also dreamed that I hurt my neck, which I did. I had to give up my job. I fall over sometimes because my leg is numb and I can feel the ghost holding me up.

Now I'm subject to depression and she's around more when I'm ill. I get hot and cold spots all through the house.

I did some research into the history of the place. Although this house is newly built, it's next to an old church and surrounded by ancient buildings so the site is very old.

If you tell her to go away, she will go. I don't feel threatened at all and everyone remarks what a nice atmosphere is here, it's comfortable and cosy.

Wow! This narrative has everything, a poltergeist, a premonition and a sighting. Usually a ghost story comprises a few of these activities, say phantom footsteps and electrical disturbances, or light bulbs popping and articles going missing, but occasionally, a story surfaces which has the whole lot. This is significant, because it shows that all these activities are not separate but linked in some way, that is, one cause could be having a variety of effects.

9. The Cotswolds

The famous yellow-tinted Cotswold stone was formed about 160 million years ago, when the Midlands was covered by a shallow sea. Most of the Cotswold Hills have a steep scarp face on one side, and a long slow climb on the other. For hundreds of years Cotswold sheep were said to produce the best wool in the world. Consequently, this is a wealthy area, with fine stone cottages and well-preserved churches.

Walking the Cotswold Way

The Cotswold Way runs for 95 miles, from Bath to Chipping Campden. It takes in Old Sodbury, Dursley, Painswick, Winchcombe, Broadway and many other picturesque Cotswold villages. The Cotswold Way goes along the steep edge of the hills.

The following was heard when chatting to customers in Maxine's Bookshop, in Pershore, Worcestershire.

> My husband and I were walking the Cotswold Way and we stayed at this farmhouse in North Nibley. I woke up in the night and there was a maid in a mob cap bending over our luggage. She was looking at the straps. I said to her, 'It's not a case, it's only haversacks' and she disappeared.
>
> The next day I went down to the reception and said, 'Can I ask you a question? Is this house haunted?' She and her husband looked at each other and said 'Why, what have you seen?' I told her about the maid. She asked, 'What room are you in?' and I told her. She told me 'You must be very sensitive because that's the only time she has appeared in that room'. They went on to say that when they first bought the house, they had some changes made and when they pulled down a certain wall there was a staircase behind it leading to a room, and in this room was the skeleton of a woman and her baby.

Curiously, this is the second account that has come our way about the same ghost in the same house. The other sighting is in *Haunted Holidays*, from a couple who were walking the Cotswold Way in 1990. The first couple described the maid as 'Young and quite innocent-looking, with a round fresh face and mob cap. She was short in stature with a dark complexion'.

Goosepimples – Saintbury Hill, near Chipping Campden

Saintbury Hill is well-known among paranormal researchers. David Taylor of Parasearch explains why:

> Many researchers suggest that reports of ghosts and other paranormal phenomena occur along what have been termed ley lines. The idea of leys came

in the last century, when a Herefordshire businessman, Alfred Watkins, noticed that ancient sites such as churches, holy wells, standing stones and hillforts appeared to be in connected by straight lines. Watkins saw these as ancient trading routes. In the 1960s the idea of leys was resurrected, but this time they were seen as lines of invisible energy connecting sacred sites. Today the idea of leys has undergone another change, one that sees them as aspects of a geomythic landscape, a connection between consciousness and the environment. Whatever leys are, there certainly appear to be a large number of anomalous phenomena reported along them. One of the most convincing leys is to be found at Saintbury in the Cotswolds. It links sites of different eras with unnerving accuracy. The ley was subject to a rigorous statistical analysis in the 1970s by mathematician Bob Forrest. The alignment proved to be significant at the 1% level – which means that it was probably deliberate.

About fifteen years ago Mavis and her husband were on holiday exploring the Cotswolds with Mavis's friend Joyce, and her husband. Mavis tells the story:

There was a party of four of us, two couples, and we were staying bed and breakfast in a farmhouse on the road towards Willesley, near the Church but on the opposite side of the road. When we arrived, our friends went into their bedroom and we went into ours. When Joyce came down to dinner, she said, 'I think my room's haunted. As soon as I walked into the room I felt very cold and had goosepimples. There's definitely something there'. She wasn't the sort of person to make things up. We were going out in the evening so we all forgot about it and went to bed.

The next morning, at breakfast, she said, 'I have seen a ghost. I woke up and felt something touching me. There was a little old lady, she had grey hair that was all untidy and she was wearing a white nightgown down to the floor and she had some teeth missing. I just lay there for a bit, watching her, then I went back to sleep.'

She said to the owner of the house, 'Is this part of the house haunted?' The owner said, 'I don't think so, I have never heard of that before'. Joyce said, 'I have seen a ghost but it was very friendly'. The owner asked, 'What did it look like?' and Joyce described it. The owner said, 'That was my mother and she died in that bedroom'.

The Sampler – Ilmington

If you climb the Ilmington Downs you are at the highest point of the county with superb views. In the late fifties or early sixties Jeanette's aunt and her husband moved into an old cottage built of Cotswold stone house in Ilmington, near Shipston-on-Stour, known as Hobdays Cottage: Jeanette says:

It was a real old thatched cottage, quite idyllic.

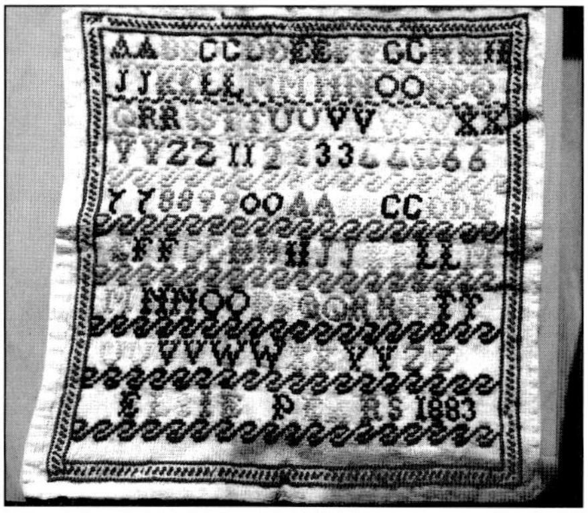

My aunt was my mum's dad's sister, we didn't see her very often as we lived in Birmingham and it was quite a jaunt out to Stratford, however I'm told that she and my mum were very close when they were young. My aunt and uncle got very rich, they made their money in cinemas, they moved to Ilmington and were very posh. Whenever we went to visit them my sister and I had to wear our Sunday best and behave ourselves.

My aunt would tell us about the ghost of a young lady who came regularly into her bedroom at night. She was beautifully dressed in a bonnet and crinoline and each time she was wearing a crinoline of a different colour. Beside her, on the floor, she always had her trousseau chest containing the clothes for her wedding, and she was very proud of it. She told my aunt that her name was Elsie Pears. This went on for many years.

I don't recall this, but I have now been told that my aunt was very fond of the gin and whenever she told my mother about the ghost, mum thought it was the gin talking. However, on one of the ghost's visits, she told my aunt that she wanted to give her proof of her past existence. She said that she had left a sampler in the loft, she had hidden it as a child and she told my aunt where it was. My aunt had never been in the loft but she went up there and found it, exactly where the ghost said it would be. The name on the sampler is Elsie Pears.

The ghost also said that she had hidden some stained glass from the local church in the garden. I don't know whether this was at the same time as she heard about the sampler, or on another visit. My aunt found the stained glass and put it in an ingle nook in the chimney breast. The ghost told my aunt that she would always be happy in the house and she was, it was a lovely house.

My uncle pooh-poohed the story until one day he heard something moving about in the loft. The loft was used to store apples and that sort of thing. He went up to investigate and there, with his own eyes, he saw the boxes of apples moving of their own accord. He believed her then.

My aunt used to tell my husband about it when we first got married. My husband never saw the ghost but he felt a presence there and we heard footsteps in the loft when there was nobody else in the house.

I don't know what the significance was of the trousseau box, whether she had been jilted as a bride or what. The sampler is really beautiful and sometimes I get it out and let my children have a look at it and tell them the story. It keeps them quiet for a while!

My aunt died when I was twelve or thirteen.

The Milkman and the Cavalier – Edgehill

One of the great ghost stories of all time comes from Edgehill. On 23rd October 1642 at Edgehill came the first great battle of the Civil War between Charles I and the Parliamentarians. Twenty-four thousand men took part and many were killed. Three months after the battle, a London printer published a pamphlet which said, 'On Saturday, - which was in Christmas time between 12 and 1 o'clock in the morning' a group of shepherds, some travellers and few local people, heard 'first the sound of drums afar off, and the noise of soldiers, as it were giving out their last groans'. The pamphlet tells how they watched the battle re-enacted in the sky for three hours, not daring to run away in case they were caught up in the fighting. When it was over, the spectators hurried to Kineton to tell Mr. Wood (the local JP) and his neighbour, Mr. Marshall (the Minister).

The next night (the Sunday before Christmas) Mr. Wood, Mr. Marshall and others went to the battlefield and were amazed to see it repeated. Rumours of it reached the King who sent a Colonel, two Captains and three high-ranking gentlemen to investigate. They stayed in Kineton until the following Saturday night, when the battle in which they had taken part was again re-enacted and they recognised several of their slain comrades.

Since then, the battle has been seen at least twice, the next year on 4th January and in the mid 1800s by a group of newspaper reporters. In more recent times, people have not seen the whole battle re-enacted but claim to have seen Prince Rupert's white charger or have heard the noise of battle. Both *Midland Ghosts and Hauntings* and *Strange Meetings* have tales from Edgehill, and every year, another strange experience comes to light, such as the following:

> I used to work for Blakes, the milk round. Early one morning, one of my mates came in as white as a sheet. He was driving up Edgehill in a van loaded with milk and he became aware of a horse and rider by the side of him. The rider was dressed just like a Cavalier, he was wearing a large hat with a fancy frock coat and carrying a sword. My mate put his foot down, but however fast he went, the Cavalier was by the side of him.

In *Midland Ghosts and Hauntings*, Barrie Roberts gives more information on the The Stone Tape theory:

> A possible explanation of some ghosts is that certain conditions impress upon the landscape a kind of recording of violent events. When a sensitive person of the right kind enters the field of the recording it will replay to them images of what has occurred. The idea was used years ago in a play called The Stone Tape by Nigel Kneale. It suggested that a combination of local electromagnetic fields and chemistry of the surroundings might cause the recording. It is an ingenious theory and one that makes more sense of hauntings like Edgehill... What is more,

there are devices that can detect the pattern of static electricity in the pile of a carpet where a foot has been pressed and left no visible outline, and we have instruments that can detect (and photograph) the thermal images of people who are no longer in a room, and cars no longer parked in a street.

The Peacock Inn – Middle Tysoe, Near Banbury

Middle Tysoe is near Meon Hill, said to have been a witches' coven, inspiring Shakespeare's three witches in *Macbeth*. Tysoe's traditional ghost is a white horse, seen in the 1900s by the postman, a policeman and the local lay preacher. It is said to be Prince Rupert's charger from the Battle of Edgehill. However, there was another phantom horse at Tysoe. In *Midland Ghosts and Hauntings*, Barrie Roberts explains:

> Until 1798 there was on a hillside a mile south of the Stratford to Banbury road at Tysoe, a figure of a horse cut out of the turf. Said to have been cut in 1461, it was supposed to commemorate the death of the Earl of Warwick's charge at the Battle of Towton on Palm Sunday that year.
>
> However, some have suggested that the figure predates the battle of Towton by a long way. The Tysoe horse was the subject (like its famous brother on the Berkshire Downs) of a scouring ceremony and festivity on Palm Sunday. It led to the area being marked on old maps as the Vale of the Red Horse for the local earth is red. Horse and festival have vanished and trees cover the site, so the outline of the Red Horse of Tysoe can only be detected by infrared aerial photography.

Locals will remember Fred and Di who were licensees of the Peacock Inn at Middle Tysoe:

> It was a lovely old building, with old oak beams and two log fires. I was told that it had once been a three-storey thatched building but they had a massive fire which destroyed the thatch. The garden was huge and in the middle was a well. It had been filled in but the top part, above the ground, was still there and it was very pretty.
>
> We had a Games Room which used to be a mortuary in Oliver Cromwell's days. In that room it was icy cold, even in summer time. It was the kind of place to go to in the middle of summer when you were boiling hot.
>
> When we first took over the pub we closed it down for a month to clear up. To celebrate the opening, we arranged a dinner for 13 people but the freezers all broke down. We had to cancel the dinner and order new freezers. The freezers were all in an outside building. I went in there and this sickly perfume nearly knocked me back. I said to the woman who was helping me, 'What on earth is that perfume you are wearing today and why have you been down to the freezers?' She said, 'I'm not wearing any perfume and I haven't been down to the freezers, it's our friendly lady' and that's when she told me the story.

There was a legend that, many years ago, a little girl fell into the well and was drowned. From time to time she came back to play in front of the fireplace in the lounge bar. One of our bar staff saw her quite regularly. Then her mother used to come looking for her, she manifested herself by a strong perfume that used to waft through the bars three or four times a day.

The perfume was so sickly that it used to make me heave. Sometimes it even went up the stairs to our flat. We had a regular who used to come in with a black Labrador and it made the dog's hackles rise.

Over the bar is a row of mugs, one on each hook, and they used to swing to and fro for no reason.

I never did see anything. My husband used to go abroad with his work for long periods and I used to think, 'If ever I see something I don't know what I'm going to do' but I never did.

The Phantom Hitch-hiker – Cheltenham

Cheltenham lies in a sheltered valley to the west of the Cotswold Hills. It owes its fame to the accidental discovery of mineral springs in 1716, the waters of which were considered to be beneficial in the treatment of gout, dyspepsia and liver complaints. The town has a famous racecourse and a prestigious Ladies' College.

No collection of ghost stories would be complete without a phantom hitch-hiker, this one is provided by Janet who lives in Churchdown:

A few years ago (since 1990), I was driving home at about 10 pm from Cheltenham. Having reached the Golden Valley Hotel, I made my way around Arle Court roundabout and took the B4063, heading for home. About 100 yards of so, in on the left, is now a small caravan park, at the roadside of which is an oldish house rendered in light grey. At the time it was slightly foggy and, as I approached the house, I perceived that I had suddenly seen a lady, in the road, waving her arms above her head. In order not to hit her I swerved around her – how I missed her was a mystery to me.

Having been in the SJAB (St. John's Ambulance brigade) I slowed down as I was duly concerned! Looking in the rear-view mirror I realised that none of the drivers behind me had taken evasive action. I was further puzzled but drove on home.

A little while later I recounted this phenomenon to my father, as we sat at the kitchen table in my home. Father had retired as a paramedic of 25 years standing having served, latterly, at the main station in Cheltenham, as a Leading Driver. He informed me that it had been one of their duties to take an elderly lady from that house to hospital – several times, in fact. He went on to say that she was now deceased and then implied that, whilst she was alive, she had been known to carry out the mode of behaviour that I had witnessed i.e. she used to try and flag down passing motorists!

10. Herefordshire And Worcestershire

The streets of Worcester have run with blood many times over the past thousand years. In 1041, the Danes came sweeping down the river Severn, sacked the town and razed the Cathedral to the ground. The story goes that one of the robbers was too greedy and tried to steal the Cathedral bell but it was too heavy, he lagged behind his comrades and was caught by the townsfolk. They flogged him until only his skin was left which they nailed to the door of the Cathedral. For centuries, a piece of skin was nailed to the door and only removed in the early twentieth century.

In the civil wars between King Stephen and Empress Matilda in the 1100s, Worcester was sacked twice. Nearly five-and-a-half centuries later, the first skirmish of the Civil War with Royalists versus Parliamentarians, took place at nearby Powick. Although the civil war finished in 1646,the son of Charles I invaded England in 1651 in the hope of regaining the throne.This led to the great Battle of Worcester which took place right across the vicinity of Worcester, but some of the fiercest fighting was in the town itself.Worcester citizens were Royalist and a large section of the Royalist army became trapped inside the city walls. One of the gates of the city was at Sidbury, and as the soldiers fled there to get away from the centre of the city they were attacked by the Parliamentarians. Estimates of the dead after the battle run to 3,000 and bodies were stacked high up against Sidbury Gate.

The victorious Oliver Cromwell ordered that the town walls be pulled down and the gates removed. So the city gates have gone, but today many of the occupants of the buildings in that area find that they still have associations with its terrible past. For example, the Commandery has a dark red stain that cannot be removed no matter how hard you scrub, said to be the blood of the Duke of Hamilton who died there during the Civil War, and a ghostly Cavalier has been seen in the cellar of the Barley Mow.

WORCESTER

A Presence for Peace

Almost opposite the Barley Mow and about 100 yards away from the Commandery is the 'Healing Touch' Complementary Health Care Centre at 4 Bath Road. For the past six years John Cartwright has been working there on a sessional basis:

> During my 23 years as a Curative Hypnotherapist I have had a number of unusual experiences.
>
> I use a small room on the first floor and on arrival the first time, I saw that all the framed professional certificates of the various therapists using that room

were displayed on one wall. I noticed that the glass of one of these was cracked. In the course of my work I regress my patients to the cause of their particular problem and so, occasionally, if the cause of their problem is in a past life, this is where they take me.

Although I do not encourage the practice, some people do sometimes ask if they can be regressed into a previous life to satisfy their own curiosity and this was the situation when I had been working here about eighteen months. A young lady, supported by a friend, had made an appointment to see me one evening, the purpose of this consultation was to ascertain the reason why she wanted to be regressed, to explain what hypnosis actually was, as opposed to what she thought it was, and to tell her something of the procedures. During the course of this discussion the 'friend' suddenly burst out, 'I don't believe in all this, its a load of nonsense, it's all made up and there are no such things as ghosts!!' With that the cracked glass fell out of the certificate on the wall and shattered on the floor. The two girls fled, and I have never seen them since. I picked up the pieces of glass and left them on the top of the desk with a note, 'I did not do this, honest!'

I duly reported this incident to the owner of the Centre and she informed me that this is a haunted property and that a number of therapists working on the first floor had heard footsteps upstairs, in the evenings, on a number of occasions. It told her that I, too, had heard these noises upstairs two or three times when I had been working late, and had been up there to check that the rooms were empty before locking up. My experiences were during the long, dark evenings.

The noises were like a slow, regular, bump, bump, bump – not too loud and I had no particular thoughts about them. At the time, I was concentrating on locking up, and I had just checked the rooms. The owner then informed me that she had investigated and found that he was a friendly ghost, a soldier, and that this was part of his patrol beat when on guard duty checking and reporting activity on the London Road bank. It was thought that this was at the time of the Battle of Worcester.

A totally different experience occurred towards the end of 2005. I was working late in the evening and was the only therapist still in the building. I was treating a male patient of about forty years of age. The room in which I work is quite small and my chair is only just inside the door which is to my right. About an hour into the treatment I became aware of someone talking quite loudly apparently outside my door, despite a large notice which is displayed requesting quiet as therapy is in progress. I assumed that one of the other therapists had come back into the building (although I had not heard the door being opened and closed) and had brought someone in with her. It was definitely a conversation, but I could only hear one lady talking, talking and talking very loudly, and getting louder, and I was beginning to get annoyed. A patient in the hypnotic state is untroubled by noise although aware of it but it was disturbing me for the first time in my 23 years experience. I was intent on what I was going and not listening to the conversation but I found it very distracting.

When the session ended the patient said that he had found the hypnotic experience interesting for he had just been having a conversation with his deceased mother and could see her too. I asked where she was, to which he replied that she had been standing just behind me, just behind my right shoulder. No wonder she was loud – she was speaking directly into the microphone of the hearing aid that I wear.

Of course, I mentioned this incident to the owner to which I received the reply, 'He must have brought that spirit with him – she is not resident here!'

The owner of the Centre, Mrs. Rita Davies, confirms his story:

I was looking for somewhere to open a healing centre. I could have opened it anywhere, but I felt drawn to this building. At that time, I didn't know that this area is swamped in military history but I felt that the area needed healing. I called the centre, 'Healing Touch' and this is where we have acupuncture, homeopathy, osteopathy, Reiki healing and other healing practices.

We moved into the building in 1995 and I knew that there was a presence here the first day we moved in. We had our children with us, they were young then, eight and six. The two little girls love open spaces where they can do cartwheels. They went into all the rooms but they refused to go into room 5. I went into the room and I felt it was very chilly, not exactly cold but prickles went up my spine. I'm a very sensitive person, I work with the Christ Consciousness, and I lit a candle, that's my symbol. I sat there quietly and waited to contact the spirit. I can't see spirits but I can feel them and I can talk to them with my mind. I was able to contact this spirit. He said he was a look-out soldier, he was keeping a lookout in that area and this building. The building is very old and has had a number of businesses in it. He said that he protects it and I must say that the chemists and the printers next to us have both had break-ins but we have always been lucky.

This is a three-storey building and in the evenings he will walk around as if he is on duty. He goes from the top to the bottom. You can hear his footsteps and hear the floor boards creaking. You can feel that someone is watching you.

He isn't frightening at all, we are all happy to work in room 5. In fact, we had someone working with homeopathy who was having difficulties with his personal relationships and he said that he always had a feeling of pure love and compassion coming from that energy.

Last year was our tenth anniversary and for this I felt that it was appropriate to invite the World Wide Peace Movement. We had these wonderful people come and light candles and they have left a memorial which says 'May peace prevail on earth' in four languages. We feel that we are putting peace back into the world and healing the past.

Barrie Roberts adds a cautionary note:'Regressions by hypnosis into 'past lives' are an extremely thorny subject. The fact of the matter is that a hypnotic subject is under a pressing urge to 'please' the hypnotist. When a hypnotist regresses someone to their childhood and asks questions, the subject's subconscious will root among its memories and see what it can rake up, but when taken back to a time when the subject did not exist the subconscious will try to please the questioner with rag-bag scraps of recollections from readings, films etc. This is why the process is so rarely capable of verification'.

Low Spirits

There have been cases where someone separates from his or her body and becomes two people. In *Midland Ghosts and Hauntings*, Betty Bates in Solihull appears to have a double' and has been seen in two places at once. These 'doubles' are sometimes known as 'Doppelgangers'. They are troublesome by tradition, always making mischief, although they have been quite docile in the few cases we have come across. Other doubles have been known world wide, the Yogi in the Himalayas claim to materialise elsewhere while they remain in their original body. This casts a new perspective on the ghost issue. If you see someone, how do you know that you're not looking at their double?

In this book are four out-of-body experiences. In the Central Birmingham section is a young girl who find herself floating above her bed, and in this chapter are an important Council official who feels himself floating, the Research Officer for Parasearch who analyses his own experiences, and a young man in Worcester who says:

> A few years ago my girl-friend and I were living in the top flat of an old house near the centre of Worcester. One night, When I was going to sleep, I felt myself going through the floorboards. I saw a chap and his girl-friend asleep in bed with the lights on and a book about the Beatles on the floor. Early next morning I knocked him up and put my head round the door. Everything was just as I had seen it including the Beatles book on the floor.

Tipstalled – The Malverns

The nine mile stretch of Malvern Hills rise suddenly from the eastern side of the flat Worcestershire plain, chiefly along the Herefordshire/Worcestershire boundary. Fifteen counties can be seen from the Herefordshire Beacon, which is nearly 1,400 feet high. On the Beacon the undulations in the hill are the remains of an enormous Iron Age fortress, said to be where the great British warrior Caracatus took a last stand against the Romans.

The Malvern Hills have long inspired writers, poets and musicians. The famous Victorian writer, Charles Grinrod featured the monk from Little Malvern Priory who was made to crawl up Raggedstone Hill every day as a punishment for his sins. He died cursing everyone upon whom the shadow of Raggedstone Hill should fall. The 14th century poetic vision, Piers Plowman, was written in the Malverns. Some of Elgar's greatest works were inspired here.

The sculptor, Oliver Webb, adds to the marvellous tales of the area:

> My father used to fly radio controlled model gliders on the Malvern Hills. North Hill was clearly visible from our house – straight down the valley. One day Dad had taken one of his gliders up on the hills, the wind was in the north, so I knew that he would be flying on North Hill. He went on his own, but usually met up with a friend or two on the hills if the conditions were good for flying. As it happened, Dad's best friend, a lovely chap called Graham, had lent me an old SLR camera (I was just getting into photography) with a couple of lenses to play with. The biggest lens was a huge old 400 mm telephoto, which when I combined it with two 2x converters went up to a whopping 1,600 mm, though the quality of the image wasn't good – also it was very difficult to hold still, even with a tripod. But I reckoned that I should perhaps be able to see Dad through this lot and set it up in the path in front of the house. In due course, a figure was visible on the hill, which I assumed to be Dad. The figure was visible against the hillside as well as in silhouette against the skyline, though when the figure moved below the skyline I was able to see the white wings of Dad's glider (it had a ten foot wingspan). When the glider was flying, I could see it particularly well against the darker hill side. After a while a second figure appeared on the skyline and moved down to join Dad a little way below the ridge.
>
> Then, as I watched, I saw the gliders wings suddenly rotate and come to a halt – in other words Dad had crashed it! What had happened was that the left wing had "tip-stalled", which means that one wing loses flying speed due to uncertain wind conditions close to the ground when flying at a relatively slow speed – the wing simply drops and if the craft is near the ground it crashes. One figure stooped down, then walked down to the plane (not actually far downhill from him), then he picked up the plane and then walked back up towards the ridge, stopping and bending down briefly at the place where the second figure still stood. Then both figures walked over the ridge (briefly very distinct in silhouette) and disappeared from view. At this point I (slightly too gleefully perhaps!) went into the house and told Mum "Dad's bust the plane, I reckon he'll be home in half an hour".
>
> Half an hour later, Dad returned with a poorly glider – I was full of the fact that I'd watched it all happen. Dad asked me if I'd taken a picture, which of course, I hadn't – the quality of the picture wasn't really all that great for a photograph, and to be honest, it hadn't really occurred to me to press the

button. Then I asked him who else was up on the hills, Dad just said that the conditions hadn't been very good and nobody else had braved it, indeed it had been so bad that that had been the probable cause of the crash. We both thought we were pulling each other's legs when I told him I'd seen the second figure. Dad assured me that he'd been completely on his own up there, since he'd even had a pee on the top of the hill and had looked around to see nobody was about! We dissected the sequence of events and everything tallied, from the way the glider crashed, to Dad stooping twice (to put down his bag and pick it back up having retrieved the wreck). The two images were definitely not an optical defect of the lens – the figures moved independently of each other, not as shadows, and there was only one glider.

For years I have been kicking myself for not having tripped the shutter that day – I'd have had photographic proof. Very tragically, Graham (who'd lent me the camera and stuff) was killed not long afterwards when his hang glider tipstalled its left wing and crashed.

Night Nurse Paralysis – Powick

This village is another part of Worcestershire with a fantastic history, partly because, at Powick, the River Teme joins the River Severn. It played a part in the war between the barons, led by Simon de Montfort and Henry III and it was here that Henry III was taken prisoner in 1264. The first skirmish of the English Civil War took place on the bridge in 1642 and nine years later it was part of the great battle of Worcester, when its fields were filled with the dead and dying. A local resident says that nearly every house in the village is haunted, even the butchers - as she was queuing for some meat an invisible force pushed her to one side. Powick had the first hydro-electric power station in Europe - unfortunately flooded in winter when it was most in demand. In 1852, Worcestershire Pauper Lunatic Asylum was opened in Powick. Six years later it had 365 patients. It was later converted into Powick Hospital. Before its closure, George Gregg, Research Officer for Parasearch, was on duty there:

In 1976 I was a second year student nurse (Registered Mental Nurse) at Powick Hospital, and was on my night duty experience on a male acute admission ward.

Because of the intense heat of the summer I had not slept properly for days and was starting to experience signs of sleep deprivation. Research shows that if you miss out on REM (Rapid Eye Movement) Sleep the body will try to catch up with it at some stage soon.

There were three phenomena that I suffered from over a few days. Firstly something called night nurse paralysis. One night I was sitting observing a patent from outside their room when the Charge Nurse came up to me and spoke. I was completely paralysed and yet I understood everything they were saying but could not answer. I must have entered a light stage of sleep but my brain had shut off my muscles, which happens to everyone in REM sleep.

The other experience a few nights later was when I could see someone getting out of bed, in the half light of the sick bay, and trying to get out through the fire escape. I thought one of the patients had got out of bed and was looking for the toilet. But when I got up to assist them they vanished before my eyes. This then repeated itself a few minutes later. This was an example of REM sleep in low light stimulus environment.

The next day when I returned to the Nurses' Rooms, before going to be to get some sleep I watched a colleague disappear and reappear before my very eyes. I was obviously having a micro sleep, so I was glad when I had finished my night duty stint and the hot weather passed over.

There's only one explanation and that's a psychological one. This could be an example of ghost-like phenomena brought on by sleep and sensory deprivation.

Swords and Guns – Evesham Hospital

There was once a great Abbey at Evesham and its remains, such as the Abbey precinct, Bishop Lichfield's tower and the Almonry, make this an attractive little town. The Almonry is now a fascinating museum with plenty of hands-on material (such as old typewriters) for children. It has long been known to be haunted. Richard Abbott lived here in the 1930s. He woke up one moonlit night, went to the window overlooking the little back garden and was just in time to see a grey monk drifting across the lawn, with his hands held as if he had a book in them.

Evesham lies in a loop of the river Avon. In 1265, the leader of a rebellion against the monarchy, Simon de Montfort, camped here in the belief that he was immune from attack. In actual fact it turned out that he was trapped and the King's armies were blocking his exits. There followed the famous Battle of Evesham, in which de Montfort's army was decimated and both he and his son were killed.

It is appropriate that, in this town famous for its battle, Dorothy should talk about a tragic war-related experience:

I was in Evesham Hospital in 1950 expecting my fourth child. This was not the happy event it should have been because, a month previously, we were living in Germany where my husband was in the army, and he was killed. He was only 33.

I was so upset when all the husbands came into the ward and were admiring their babies that the nurses moved me upstairs into the adult ward, two floors up.

I was lying in bed when I saw a man looking in through the window from the outside. I realised it was my husband, but he wasn't in uniform, he was wearing his favourite jacket. I saw him quite clearly, only from the head to the waist because of the window frame, looking in through the window. I could not believe it. I said to the nurse, 'There's a man at the window!' She replied, 'Oh, that's impossible, he'd need a ladder to get up here'.

I had been feeling very bitter but after that I felt a lot calmer. I think he came along to make sure I was alright.

Out of My Body – Sedgeberrow, Evesham

How intriguing to find a paranormal expert having an out-of-body experience. Here is George Gregg's account and his analysis:

In 1973 when I was 18, and still living with my parents in Churchill Road, I had an unusual experience. I normally went out with my mates to the pub (and so on) as many country lads did at that time, but one night I felt shattered and decided to stay in and go to bed early. At about 1.00 am I found myself suspended from the living room ceiling. As I looked down I could see the embers burning in the grate. I could see the T.V. on the sideboard. I could see my mother's tablets that she took for her legs and there was loose change scattered over a newspaper. Also I saw a small stub of a pencil and a crossword partially completed.

Strangely I came to the conclusion that I was out of my body and I panicked. I felt as if I was being sucked through a tunnel and I woke up in bed shouting out, fortunately, my mother and my father did not stir. I crept downstairs and as I was entering the living room I turned on the electric light. Everything was as I had seen it, except that it wasn't from the vantage point of the ceiling. This experience was so vivid that it has remained with me all my life. Since that time I discovered that others call this an 'Out-of-body experience', or 'astral travel'. I borrowed books out of the library and tried to reproduce it but to no avail. I have had one or two other OBE since then, but it has always been random and uncontrolled by me.

Paranormal Explanation: From a paranormal perspective this is an Out of Body Experience (OBE) where the mind/soul/astral body is thought to separate from the body and go on its travels either through the Earth, invisible to our fellow humans, or through the Astral Plane, another dimension parallel to the Earth, where the spirits are thought to live.

Psychological Explanation: A more rational explanation is that this experience is a lucid dream, which usually happens when the dreamer is in a light stage of sleep and finds it difficult to tell if they are awake or asleep.

Emma Vernon Rises Again – Hanbury

Nearly every book about Worcestershire ghosts features a sighting of Emma Vernon. She has been seen by a number of people including a local lady taking her dog for a walk, a solicitor's assistant who explores old churches, a young man waiting outside the nearby Country Girl public house, and several drivers.

Emma was born in 1755, she was an only child and the great grand-daughter of Sir Thomas Vernon, who built the family home, Hanbury Hall. When Emma was in her early twenties she was married to Henry Cecil of the aristocratic Cecil family but when she had only been married three years she eloped to Portugal with the local curate. Her husband, Henry Cecil, bigamously married a farmer's daughter and when he later inherited the title Marquise of Exeter, the farmer's daughter found she had become a Countess. Known as the 'Cottage Countess', she was very famous. Emma's curate died in Portugal of consumption, Emma returned to Hanbury but she was now almost penniless and when she asked a local solicitor, John Philips to sort out her affairs he married her. However, her curate was her one great love and when she knew she was dying she asked to be buried in the blanket in which she had nursed him. She is buried in unconsecrated ground at her request so she lies on the outskirts of Hanbury Churchyard.

Tess is a reliable, responsible young lady in public service. She reports:

A few years ago I was going from the Bromsgrove side of the Hanbury Road to the Eagle and Sun to meet a group of friends. My sense of navigation is hopeless – I have lived here all my life! – I had got lost and I was late.

I was driving from the Hanbury Turn towards Hanbury itself. In front of me was another car, a mini, which I was catching up rapidly. Just short of the Country Girl is a road junction and we were by there when I saw the brake lights go on. I thought, 'Why is it braking on this straight country road?' Then I saw that going towards the middle of the road from the far side was a ghost.

When I first saw her I immediately thought, 'milkmaid', That was my immediate impression but what she was actually wearing was a bonnet, shawl and a long skirt – all woollen – and clogs. I have been trying to remember why I was so sure that she was wearing clogs. If it had been a modern person I would have described her shoes as wellies. She was slate grey all over – it was like looking at a graphite drawing where you are able to see all the pencil lines round the edges. I was watching her for less than half a minute – just the time it took to get across the road. At the time, it seemed like an hour.

The car in front of me accelerated away. I am sure that the driver had seen it. The apparition then drifted across the road and disappeared. It could have gone through the hedge but it disappeared by degrees, it melted away.

When I passed the line that had been taken by the ghost the temperature in the car plummeted. When I got to my friends I was wearing a fake fur coat and gloves but my hands were frozen.

In a funny way, I was actually quite pleased. I thought, 'Ye Gods, there is a real ghost!' I was only disappointed that the people I was going to meet hadn't seen it. I knew they would have given their eye teeth to see it. When we had finished our meal we went back there, just in case, but of course, it had gone.

Keeping the Light On – Droitwich

Droitwich sits on a great salt lake and until recent times provided the salt for most of the county and beyond.The Romans recognised the value of the 'white gold' and established a settlement here, providing many a Roman spectre in the town. Perhaps the best example comes from a young man who was stock-taking one night at his place of work when he and his colleague spotted a Roman soldier at the far end of the workshop.They rushed to catch what they thought to be an intruder but no-one was there.

Robert was only 12 when he saw his ghost in 1983. He says it feels like a long time ago.As it was only a black shape no-one knows whether or not it was another Roman:

> I was staying at a friend's house in Coldfield Walk in the Copcut estate in Droitwich. It had only been up for a few years and was previously farmland, I can remember walking over the fields in 1981.We stayed up for a long time watching videos, then we decided that we would sleep in the living room, so we laid our sleeping bags on the living room floor. About two o'clock in the morning we turned out the lights and got into our sleeping bags. We both dozed off. I probably slept for about 20 minutes. I woke up and distinctly saw a tall dark figure walk from the living room door to where the T.V. was at our feet, that is, up to the end of our sleeping bags. It was a tall, dark figure, solid-black with no features and without a sound. I wasn't frightened, just sleepy and I closed my eyes.Ten minutes later I woke up again and it occurred to me what had happened. I woke up my friend and asked him if he had been out of his sleeping bag at any time. In any case, my friend was sleeping right next to me and I would have felt him if he had got out at all. It couldn't have been my friend's mother or father because the door was closed and he walked from the door across the room. I would have heard him open the door.
>
> We both spent the rest of the night with the light on.

The Poltergeist – Redditch

Redditch is usually thought of as a new town but in actual fact, it was founded in 1138 by a group of Cistercian monks who founded a great abbey. It became one of the richest abbeys in England and played a part in events of national importance. The town grew around the abbey, then moved up the hill. Bordesley Abbey was already in a poor state by the time Henry VIII dissolved the monasteries and it has now completely disappeared except for bumps and hollows in the Bordesley Abbey meadows. The local Forge Mill museum and Visitor's Centre gives its history including that of its famous ghost - Guy of Warwick, known as the Black Dog of Arden, who was buried here in 1313 (see the Warwick section) and apparently manifests himself as a black dog.

From the 1700s onwards Redditch became famous for its needles, springs and fish-hooks. Then in the 1960s it was designated as a new town to take the Birmingham overspill and the population doubled. The next story comes from a family in Greenlands, one of the new housing developments:

We've had a problem or two over the past couple of years but until recently, it has been nothing to worry about. Most months we have had some kind of poltergeist activity.

The week before last Christmas we went to Plymouth. We wanted to do some family history so we had to go on the Friday when the place was open so I couldn't do my usual Friday shopping in Redditch. So I bought three packs of Anchor butter in Plymouth (my husband is allergic to dairy food and it's the only butter or margarine he can take). On the Wednesday, I looked in the fridge – now, we had used one packet so there should have been two in there but they had disappeared. When my husband came home from work I said to him, 'We did get three packs didn't we?' I had hardly anything in the fridge and he could see that they had completely disappeared. He blamed it on to me and said, 'Oh, it must be you'. The next morning he got up and went to make his breakfast and there they were, not in the door where I usually put them but on the bottom shelf.

It was the same with Branston pickle. I put that in the door. I went to do his sandwiches and it wasn't there. I thought, 'I must have put it in the cupboard or my husband had put it somewhere'. His parents came on the Thursday night and I was telling his mum about it. Friday morning, it was back in the fridge again.

We have have a German Shepherd. He's a lovely dog, really sloppy. When we go up to bed at night he lies in the bedroom next to the bed but as soon as we turn the lights off he goes downstairs. That has been happening for all the seven years he has been with us. Now, over the last six months we will turn the lights off, instead of going downstairs, she goes and sleeps in the bathroom. She has never slept upstairs until now. The first time it happened my husband said that he couldn't open the bathroom door, something was blocking it behind and it was the dog. It was as if someone had shut her in the bathroom. The door is never shut. We call the bathroom the dog's bedroom now!

Just before Christmas my dog was acting strangely. He kept looking behind and whimpering, and he wouldn't settle. I had purchased a tree of lights from a nursery – a Christmas tree with lights on it. It looked so pretty in the hall. With it came two spare bulbs that I put in the dresser in the hall. One of the bulbs went, which meant that the tree wouldn't work and it was such a shame. I looked for the two bulbs but I couldn't find them. I left it for four or five days, then my husband came upstairs one morning and said, 'I think you should come downstairs, and have a look at something'. You will never believe this, but the tree was all lit up.

> Just lately one or two things have happened that are really worrying and quite frightening. Last night I washed up and put everything away and slotted the bread knife into the knife container.Then when I came down in the morning the knife flew out of the container on to the floor and narrowly missed the dog's foot. If it had gone into the dog's foot it would have also gone into mine. Also, the kettle had moved itself to the other side of the kitchen.
>
> I'm convinced that there is something in the house.

Whether or not there is something in the house is anyone's guess until more research has been carried out on the poltergeist phenomenon. As we have stated previously, electrical disturbances are very common in poltergeist activity, usually it's light bulbs popping, the television or the kettle switching itself on and off, problems with the telephone and so on. Poltergeists also seem attracted to food. It's usually the sweet things that go missing, the marmalade or the sugar.There's one small office with a poltergeist where they get through a bag of sugar a day!

Shadows at Foxlydiate

Foxlydiate is a tiny hamlet off the A448 Bromsgrove Highway between Bromsgrove and Redditch, on the edge of the Redditch conurbation. It has a hotel, a service station and a few houses.To the north is Hewell Grange, once the seat of Lord Windsor but now a Remand Centre and graced by two prisons in its grounds.To the northwest is Tardebigge Church, the spire of which can be seen for miles around, and at its foot the ground drops away to the Worcester and Birmingham canal and 58 locks, one of them perhaps the deepest lock in England.

A local resident remarked,'The whole area is brimming with ghosts'. Locals have seen a 'flying hearse' and the 'white lady of the Foxlydiate' is well-known. Workmen plastering a well in the Foxlydiate Hotel were amazed when a woman's face kept appearing in the plaster.The hotel has a resident ghost, an old coachman named Tom. Next door to the Foxlydiate Hotel is the Service Station where Susan* works:

> These 'happenings' were at the time of the refurbishment at the end of 2004. Things went missing, usually things I need to use like the diary or the more important fuel delivery certificate book. One of my duties is to oversee fuel deliveries. During one of these deliveries the night porter from the Foxlydiate Hotel came for the newspapers and he was accompanied by a dark shadow. When the night porter arrived on the forecourt the fuel delivery meter went berserk, the tanker driver could not calculate how much fuel was being pumped because the meter was going backwards and forwards. As soon as the night porter left to go back to the hotel the shadow went with him and the petrol meter returned to normal, however at about half distance the

shadow turned and came back across the forecourt and the petrol meter went berserk again. The shadow passed from the forecourt and once again the petrol meter settled down.

One day, I saw a figure by the door standing in front of the fridge. There were other people in the shop with me but no-one else could have seen it as they were walking through it. They would have had to walk round the figure to get in and out of the shop. It did un-nerve me, a chill went up my back and my hair stood on end.

On another occasion we were having the works' Christmas meal at the Foxlydiate Hotel and my daughter came with us. She went off to the toilets and came back almost running. She was in the toilets by herself when the hand drier turned on – she hadn't got as far as using it so it hadn't been activated by her. Also she heard the toilet doors opening, closing and locking themselves, and the taps being turned on and off by themselves.

The Foxlydiate Hotel stands on the site of Foxlydiate house, and where the garage is now used to be the herb garden. I understand the owners used to enjoy sitting in the garden. I think that is who I see although I can't be certain.

This is another of those many stories where the alterations, additions or refurbishment of a building seems to unleash something out of the brickwork and strange things start happening. If you start knocking your home about, be prepared!

Squashing a Ghost – Wychbold

Although Wychbold is predominantly rural, it has two famous landmarks, Webbs Garden Centre and the 700 foot high masts of the BBC transmitting station near Droitwich. The Church and many of the cottages were built by John Corbett, the Salt King, who developed an efficient method of salt production in the 1860s and revived the salt works around Droitwich. He also built the nearby Chateau Impney. On the road outside a tall, thin, dark figure wearing a double-breasted coat down to the ground is sometimes seen on dark and rainy nights hitching a lift but when willing motorists stop he has disappeared. Another strange figure apparently haunts the country roads. Brian related the following incident on a radio programme with Ed Doolan in 2002:

I had the distinct honour of running over a ghost. I worked some years ago in my youth at Upton Warren farm, Wychbold, Bromsgrove, and I was going to early morning milking at about 4 o'clock in the morning down the lane and all of a sudden I saw this little old man walk in front of the car and I ran him over.

Of course, you can imagine, in a panic I got out the car and he had gone! Late in the day, after we had finished the milking, I mentioned it to the bloke around the farm and he said, 'Oh yes, that was Mr. So-and-so who used to live in the little cottage in the trees over the field. One day he was walking down the lane, not used to cars, and he got run over'.

Evidently he comes back to get run over every now and again! He's probably got nothing better to do!

David Taylor of Parasearch states:

Some of our earliest and most scary ghost reports involve haunted roads. Ever since roads have been built, they have been places to encounter the supernatural. There are a huge amount of reports that are termed 'Phantom Hitch-Hiker', where people claim to have unsuspectedly, either given a lift to a ghost or accidentally run one over! In many instances the figure seems physically real, making the experience even more distressing. One of the most famous types of this ghost is centred around Blue Bell Hill in the south of England. Witnesses have come forward to report encountering both a beautiful girl and an ugly old hag on the same stretch of road. There are also many reports in the Midlands of haunted stretches of road – so be careful who you pick up!

In *Ghosts, Murders and Scandals of Worcestershire* is a horrifying story by Mr. Raymond from Upton-on-Severn who seems to have picked up an out-of-body phantom.

BROMSGROVE

Bromsgrove is generally thought of as an old nail-making town, but it was established long before the industrial revolution. The archives have many ancient tales and the town even has a medieval legend incorporated into its coat of arms as a boar! In the British museum is the Ballad of the Jovial Hunter, going back to the time of Henry VIII. It tells how Sir Ryalas went hunting and came across a distraught woman who said that a wild boar had killed her husband and thirty of his men. Sir Ryalas blew his horn to all four points of the compass, the boar emerged and after a fierce battle, the boar was killed. Instead of being grateful, the woman flew at him and said that she had changed her son into a boar, in order to kill Sir Ryalas. The latter recognised her as a witch and split her head in two with his axe. Not a nice story but to medieval taste.

Aunty's Apparition

The Primrose Hospice in Bromsgrove relies entirely on voluntary contributions. Hard-working volunteers organise events ranging from a Luncheon Club and a choir to a lottery. Donations for the lottery are collected by Kay Hadley whose grandfather, Herbert, William Perry, laid the foundation stone to Redditch Baptist Church in Easemore Road. Kay says:

I believe in ghosts because my aunty, Iris Perry, saw one.

My aunty is now in her eighties and until 1966 she lived in Glover Street in Redditch, then she and my uncle retired to a modern bungalow near Newquay.

For the first twelve months or so they felt cold spots in the house and heard strange noises. They could hear music but, whichever room they were in, the music seemed to come from another room. They didn't believe in ghosts and it never occurred to them that they could be experiencing something paranormal. It was not until their son, who was on a visit, was having a pee in the bathroom when he felt a coldness on his neck and he turned round to see a large ball of white mist, from which the coldness seemed to be emanating. The couple then realised that something unusual was happening. They were able to identify the music with the cold spots in the house.

One night, my aunty woke up in the middle of the night and saw an old seaman standing by the side of the bed. He had a beard, a woolly hat and a woolly jumper and he was standing there looking at them. She could only see him down to his waist. She woke my uncle, who took one look at the apparition, grabbed her hand and said, 'We're not staying here'. They jumped out of bed, threw on some clothes and in the early hours of the morning, knocked up my aunty's sister (who is my mother) who lived nearby. Early the next morning they went to see the local vicar.

The house was exorcised and all sorts of things but they wouldn't live there. They moved to another area in Cornwall.

Advice from a Ghost

Here is George Gregg again, the Research Officer for Parasearch, with more thought-provoking narratives:

In 1984 a colleague of mine, let's call him Michael, who suffered from alcoholism, took to coming up my drive after last orders and falling over my rubbish bins. My wife started to get annoyed with his behaviour. Sometimes I would spend a little time sobering him up with coffee and then giving him assistance over the back fence into his garden, it backed onto half of my garden. I would watch him until he staggered up to his place, got in through the side door and turned his kitchen light on.

I was working in a local NHS Mental Health Unit and news arrived one day that Michael had died in the most gruesome of circumstances. Apparently he choked to death on food and whisky. Not long afterwards I transferred to another Mental Health Unit nearer my home where long-stay patients with schizophrenia were being rehabilitated for life in the community.

At that time my wife was taken ill and the doctor that I called thought she may be suffering from a miscarriage so she had to go to hospital (Bromsgrove

General). Meanwhile I arranged for my 18-month old daughter to go and stay with her grandparents for a few days.

It was a Sunday morning and I was due to go to work mid-day. I was just waking up, in that hypnogogic state halfway between sleep and waking when I saw Michael standing in my bedroom. He said,'George, I want you to get a book called Theosophy by Rudolph Steiner'. Of course I wanted to ask what he meant but unfortunately he was gone. I was a bit hazy about what he said, I couldn't remember Steiner's first name.

In the afternoon I was having a group meeting with my clients, one of which had been admitted the day before. He was introducing himself to the others and explained that years ago he had attended a Rudolph Steiner School. This of course broke my dream and I asked him had he ever heard of a book called 'Theosophy'? He hadn't but he described the school's headmistress and her belief in reincarnation. The nurse who was on duty noticed how the colour drained out of my face having been confronted with this coincidence.

The next day I was on an early shift and on the way to visit my wife in hospital I dropped into the local library and in the ten million to one chance that I would find this book, I asked them, had they got a book called 'Theosophy' by Rudolph Steiner? To my greatest shock, after spending a while rummaging around, they came up with it. Naturally I asked if I could borrow it and I took it away with me. I went to visit my wife then went home to read this book.

The book was about the afterlife, the astral plane and the stages that individuals go through (allegedly) after they die. Despite the amazing coincidence of a dead man, in a dream, recommending a book to me that I have no recollection of hearing about or having read before, I unfortunately did not find what it had to say very believable or credible.

Paranormal explanation: To take this experience at face value (1) Michael was trying to tell me about the afterlife in a dream (2) I missed the message so it was reinforced in a client meeting. There seems to be elements of synchronicity (coincidences based upon the stream of consciousness).

Psychological explanation: The most likely explanation is that I had heard about the book before (cryptomnesia). Michael may have even told me about it when he was alive but I was not paying attention or simply forgot about it until my unconscious dredged it up at a time of stress (my wife being admitted to hospital).

Ghostly Dogs and Other Phantoms – Lickey End, near Bromsgrove

George Gregg has lived at Lickey End, near Bromsgrove, for many years and although it's near junction 1 of the M5, only a short drive takes you to the top of the lovely Lickey Hills. Before most people had a car, a tram ride to the Lickey Hills was a day-out treat for Birmingham folk.

We have enough sightings of ghostly animals to fill a book in its own right. Phantom white horses are seen across the Midlands. A ghostly hedgehog scuttles across a kitchen in Leamington. Many dog and cat owners are convinced their pet visits them after death. In Studley, a phantom cat (not theirs) settles on the children's bed, they can't see it but there is an indentation in the bedclothes and they can hear it purring. Consequently, George Gregg's proposed explanations will be of interest to many people:

> I have had a series of nocturnal experiences reminiscent of ghostly phenomena and the following gives an overview of the most common ones:
>
> I have experienced a range of prods, pokes, tickles, sometimes relentless for minutes at a time, giving me the impression that someone was teasing me at night. Often I would feel that I was paralysed and sometimes had the experience of being held down. I also experienced waking up to see the fading shape of a human form. They always happened when sleeping alone. These experiences seemed very real and convincing to me.
>
> Ghost Dog (1) (2001): I woke up about 3.00 am on morning and I saw my long dead dog (1992) with her head on my pillow. She was a black Labrador/collie cross called Lettice.
>
> The amazing thing was that I could see her eyelashes and her chest was moving up and down as if asleep. I fell asleep and it was only in the morning I realised I had witnessed something unusual.
>
> Ghost Dog (2) (2002): I awoke sometime in the night to be aware, I am not sure how, of one of my other dead dogs Plum, daughter of Lettice (1998) leaning against me in the bed. I could feel her furry ears. Again I fell asleep thinking nothing of it until I woke the next day.
>
> Ghost Dog (3) (2003): I have also had similar experiences to those above with Snoopy, a dog I inherited off my Father in 1992, which died in 1999.
>
> *Paranormal Explanation:* That all three dogs had visited me from the spirit world and that the non-specific pokes and prods could be attributed to some mischievous spirit.
>
> *Psychological, Physiological Explanation:* All of these could be attributed to; sleep paralysis, apnoea (breathing ceases for a short time), or hypnogogic hallucinations (between waking and sleeping).

Septic Tanks and Floating Bodies – Hartlebury

The Bishop of Worcester's castle is here, it has been occupied by successive bishops for four centuries. To go through the Bishops of Worcester would take a whole book in itself. They have been confidants of kings and queens and taken part in national events. Some were feted and over-indulged while others were neglected, starved and even imprisoned. Two were burned at the stake. Their portraits are in the Great Hall which is open to the public. There's a famous library here, donated by Bishop Hurd and locals say that Bishop Hurd's wife has frequently been seen floating across the top of the entrance drive. No-one knows why it should be the wife that appears and not the Bishop, nor why she chooses this particular spot.

John* is an intelligent, sensible individual who was employed by Wychavon Council in 1974. For the next six years he had a series of most unusual experiences:

> It's happened to me a number of times, always in the open air and always at work. I'm talking to somebody, usually about septic tanks or water supplies, then suddenly I'm aware that I'm floating nine or ten feet above my head. My body is still down there and it's still talking to the person down on the ground but I'm up above, looking down on the top of the other person's head. I'm not taking any notice of the rest of the environment and just concentrating on the one person I'm talking to. After a few minutes I come down. The person I was speaking to never noticed anything wrong. Nothing really happened except to me.
>
> It's happened ten or twelve times. I would forget about it in the hectic demands of the day-to-day work, then a few months or weeks later the experience would be repeated.
>
> I have a feeling that it always happened in the Hartlebury area.

Here we have another out-of-body experience, interesting because it's witnessed by another person who doesn't notice anything unusual.

HEREFORDSHIRE

Herefordshire is now a peaceful, rural county but there was a good deal of fighting here after the Norman conquest of 1066 and Hereford was an important place, much of the land being held by the powerful Lords Marchers. Having been a border county, Hereford is full of castles, the chief being Richard's Castle, Clifford, Weobley, Hereford, Wilton, Goodrich and Wigmore.

All the Midland counties have memorable churches but perhaps Herefordshire has the most notable. To begin with, there's the marvellous cathedral, begun in 1079 and containing the Mappa Mundi - the earliest known map of the world. Many of the modest churches - even the smaller ones - have the advantage of containing carvings from the Herefordshire School. The movement lasted from about 1130 to 1180 and was originally an entire school of art, creating stone-glass window, effigies, wall paintings, wooden carvings, and stone sculptures but only the sculptures have survived. Kilpeck is the most complete example but there are carvings by the School in Eardisley, Castle Frome, Fownhope, Brinsop, Stretton Sugwas and many other churches.

In for the Chop! – Bromyard

Some experts believe that the spectacular north and south doorways of St. Peter in Bromyard are also the work of the Herefordshire School. This busy little village on the Herefordshire/Worcestershire border was home to Eric, the butcher, older residents will remember him. He probably joked with his customers about the ghost and here is the full story, told by Eric:

> I had a butcher's shop in Broad Street, Bromyard, for 37 years. The three-storey house was over 200 years old. When I first moved in, the ground floor was the shop and flat, downstairs was a converted cellar while the owner of the shop lived on the top floor.
>
> While I was working downstairs in the converted cellar I would look up the stairs and catch a glimpse of someone waiting to be served. I would run up but no-one would be there. I remember once I was standing at the butcher's block in the cellar (where you cut the meat up) and I looked up to see a man standing at the counter. He was thin and not very tall, in his twenties or thirties and with an old tweed jacket and trousers. He looked like a typical farmer. I went up to serve him but he had gone.
>
> I persuaded the owner of the property to have a house built on the site of the old slaughterhouse, so she moved out of the flat upstairs into the house and my son moved into the flat. While he was there, he had several strange experiences. The doors had great heavy old locks and were always locked and bolted at night. When he and his wife were in bed, they would hear the bolts being pulled back and there would be the sound of heavy, hob-nailed boots coming up the stairs. They would come right up to the third floor. One Sunday morning he and his girlfriend were waiting for his brother to arrive who was paying them a visit and didn't know the area, when they heard a voice calling his girlfriend's name, very clearly, twice. She rushed to the window but there wasn't a soul in the street.
>
> In 1973, a fire burned everything. When it was rebuilt, I had the cellar tiled and baker's ovens put in, together with a butcher's block and a refrigerator block. I specialised in pies and distributed them over a 50-mile radius every day. When I left in 1996, English Heritage restored the front to how it looked 200 years ago.

Horror at Little Hereford

First published in *Unquiet Spirits of Worcestershire* in 1999, we thought this was too good a story to let rest and have repeated it below.

A tiny track leads to Little Hereford Church off the A456 between Tenbury Wells and Woofferton. The tower is thirteenth century with a pyramid roof and inside the church is one of the best-preserved set or rood stairs in the county.

In the meadow beyond the churchyard are interesting-looking bumps and ridges. Terry Hill, a member of the local historical society, said:

> Some of the members of the Tenbury Wells and District Civic and Historical Society had done some research on a site in Little Hereford, at the back of the fortified church. I think it was in 1993 that we were asked by the Worcestershire Archaeological Society to lay on an open day. Three or four of us went from the Society and we took some ladies whom we intended to train to act as guides on the day. It was a very hot summer evening in August and we were all in our shirt sleeves. The site is little more than a series of platforms, we were walking along these and I was showing them where everything had been, when one of the ladies suddenly clutched my arm so fiercely that her nails bit into my skin and the hair on her arms stood up on end. She cried, 'Please get me away from this terrible place'. She was in a dreadful state. She said that she could see the roofs of thatched cottages on fire and women and children being mutilated and butchered. Her husband was in another group so we called him over and he said, 'Oh yes, she's psychic'. She was so upset that she has since left our society.
>
> When she described the scene she mentioned two towers, one each side of the site. The following day we scratched about in the soil and we found the remains of a circular tower on one side. The other side is now under the river but there was a lot of dressed stone in the bank which suggests a building of some kind was there.
>
> We looked into the history of the site and found that the Welsh raided the area several times. AG Bradley, in his book In the March and Borderland of Wales (published in 1905 by Constable), writes that they had once caught the people before they could get into the church. They put the village to the torch, butchered the children and raped the women. Also, according to Thomas Habington, the Elizabethan Historian, the Danes are known to have 'ravenously sacked' this area.

The Bad-tempered Ghost – Hereford Cathedral

Hereford Cathedral could be described as the jewel in the County's crown. The first Cathedral was built in the first half of the 1100s but was burned down, not by the marauding Danes, but by the Welsh. It was rebuilt in the 1140s and some of this early work still survives, although most of the building dates back to the 13th and 14th centuries. The cathedral later suffered two major calamities: the western tower fell in 1786 and a little over a hundred years later the Victorians decided to renovate the building. It has a great tourist attraction - the quaint Mappa Mundi one of the earliest known maps of the world. It was the work of Richard de Bello, treasurer of Lincoln Cathedral, and was made shortly after 1280.

One of the other stone masons saw a figure standing up there in broad daylight, silent and very still.

For many years Oliver Webb worked as a stonemason (latterly in stained glass as well) on various churches. It was Oliver who gave us the story of Worcester Cathedral and here he tells us about the ghost of Hereford Cathedral:

Most churches and cathedrals have nooks and crannies where the public never go. Hereford Cathedral, for example has a spiral stair in each corner of the tower, only one is still accessible, but the other three still exist and although blocked of at the top and bottom, can be accessed by scrambling around the outside of the bell-ringing chamber. The triforium was bisected when the Lady Chapel roof was raised at some stage and a higher arch inserted below – there remain two short sections of passageway blanked off at both ends which can only be found if you climb inside the roof space and scramble through a very little hole in the wall on the east side. It is completely black in there – no light whatsoever! In the south transept are those lovely Norman triforium which can be accessed from the stair in the N/E corner of the transept. These are very visible from the ground, but inaccessible to the public – yet whilst I was working there in about 1990 one of the other stone masons saw a figure standing up there in broad daylight, silent and very still.

On one occasion I was with my colleague at Hereford Cathedral, we were to take details of the glass in the little room above the north porch (they are some lovely old diamond pane leaded lights). The room (actually two little rooms, though only one has windows) is only accessible nowadays through a little door in the north aisle, and up a winding stair. We went to the verger and got the key (a massive iron thing), we were told on no account to lose the key, and to lock ourselves in and out each time. I'd previously done a lot of work at Hereford, so was very familiar with this routine – to prevent people wandering where they are not supposed to.

Originally there had been access to the room from outside via a pair of spiral stairs either side of the north porch's main entrance arch, but these doors have been locked and unused for years (at the time of this event, they were also barricaded with hoarding). My colleague and I went up to the room and took a lot of measurements, drawings and photographs for our report on the glazing. Then at around lunch time we thought we'd go up into town to get some sandwiches and drop our films at the shop to be developed "on the hour" so that better ones could be taken in the afternoon if necessary. We left all our clobber in the room and duly locked ourselves out of the room, pocketed the only key and went up into town. Later, upon our return, we discovered all of our stuff strewn around the room as if someone had hurled it everywhere. Cameras and tools everywhere. Nothing was missing and nothing broken – just scattered. In fact I took my wife there the following Saturday to take a couple of extra details and we were still finding pencils and cigarette papers all around the place!

Veteran researcher and investigator Paul Devereux makes a very valid point when he says: "It might therefore be best for us to not totally disbelieve in the reality of spirits and yet not automatically assume that they are simply the ghosts of the dead or beings from the Otherworld either. They may be a part of a reality for which our culture does not yet have working concepts".

Look Back in Anger – Shobdon

One of the greatest criminal acts in art history was perpetrated at Shobdon in the middle of the 1700s by the Lord of the Manor, Hon Richard Bateman. He pulled to pieces a fantastic, carved church dating back to the 1140s, in the same style as Kilpeck but superior in size and construction, and rebuilt it in the Rococo style. True, it's a pretty church, much admired and worth a visit but the marvellous arches of the Herefordshire School are up a grassy slope 100 yards away and so weathered that the carvings are difficult to make out. Fortunately, a plaster cast of the tympanum survives in the Victoria and Albert museum.

Like the blacksmith in Birmingham, stonemason and sculptor Oliver Webb has a collection of ghost stories:

> My wife and I rented a cottage at Shobdon, for a year. The house wasn't all that old or anything special – just a nice '50s style 3 bed detached home. One daylight evening as we sat watching television in the downstairs room there came the most enormous crash – right in front of us, between us and the television. It was preceded momentarily by a slight slithering sound. We both nearly jumped out of our skins. A few minutes later a second crash came from the hallway. The noises definitely were inside the house, the first was only about five feet in front of us. The floors were wooden with carpet on (no cellar) and nobody else was in the house. The size of the crash suggested a weight similar to a hundredweight bag of cement being dropped from head height onto the wooden floor – it was big. I'm very familiar with the sort of creaks and bumps buildings make when they cool down (having been in churches at night working on my own has shown me that to good effect) and these crashes were way beyond that sort of noise. Oddly, neither of us remember feeling any sort of impact through the floorboards. I immediately went all round the house, inside and out, but we never got any kind of a clue as to what it was we heard.

It's curious that a sculptor should have an experience such as this in a place where a monumental ancient sculpture was desecrated. Could there be any connection?

11. SHROPSHIRE

This lovely county is bordered by Wales to the West and Herefordshire to the south. Within its perimeters are the Clee Hills, the Breidden Hills, Wenlock Edge and the Wrekin and it is watered by the river Severn and its tributaries. The only large town is Telford and among the smaller towns are Shrewsbury and Ludlow, considered to be among the most photogenic in the Midlands. Ludlow is second only to London in its reputation for good food. Shropshire is chiefly an agricultural county although there was a coalfield in Coalbrookdale, which, together with Ironbridge, claims to have kick-started the industrial revolution.

Shropshire is rich in history, it has been involved in the Romano-British wars, and it figured prominently in the wars against the Welsh. A great battle was fought in Shrewsbury in 1403 when the Percy family, led by Sir Henry Percy (Shakespeare's 'Hotspur') rebelled against the king. Hotspur was killed, his followers fled and 1,600 lay dead or dying. Ludlow was fiercely Royalist and its castle was destroyed in the Civil War of 1646 by the Parliamentarians. Five years later a house in Shropshire sheltered a fugitive king.

Still Searching – Boscobel House

Boscobel House lies on the Staffordshire and Shropshire border. In the grounds is a famous tree, a descendant of the Royal Oak where, in 1651, the future Charles II escaped the soldiers by hiding in an oak tree. The battle of Worcester had been lost and Charles was on the run for six weeks with an enormous price on his head. The house is open to the public where you can see the tree and hear tales of the old priest holes, built to hide Roman Catholic priests from Oliver Cromwell's men. The house has therefore been searched many times, in the 1500s and 1600s for Roman Catholic priests and in 1651 for the escaping Charles.

Here is another story from Kerry, the alarms expert who is often called out under mysterious circumstances:

> I will tell it just as I remember it. Now the house is fitted out from top to bottom with alarm sensors and cameras for security, and the custodian lives on site in accommodation that adjoins the house.
>
> The following has happened quite a few times over the years usually in the winter time and in the early hours of the morning, and always follows the same pattern.
>
> It starts off with the sensor in the attic of the house being activated which shows up on the panel in the custodian's accommodation. From this panel he can see pictures from all the cameras and keep an eye on any movement in the

house with the alarm sensors. Then the next light on the panel comes on and the next, but nothing can be seen on the cameras, yet something is setting off the alarm sensors. This continues throughout the whole of the house as if someone is coming down from the attic through the rooms of the house, but still nothing can be seen by the cameras. As the lights come on on the panel, it is clear that whatever-it-is is making its way down through the house until it reaches the bottom floor then loud banging can be heard on a wall, the other side of which is the custodians bedroom.

When things have stopped and the lights in the house have been put on, the custodian goes round the house checking things but nothing can be found, all doors and windows are locked and no explanation can be found.

Given that this is a Roman Catholic house with a priest hole, and also that King Charles hid here, could the events be that of someone conducting a top to bottom search of the house?

I'm Keeping an Eye On You! – Telford

In the 1960s it was obvious that a vast new town was necessary to house the overspill from the Black Country. A site seven miles east of Shrewsbury was chosen, old towns and villages were linked by a fast road and infilled by new developments, with a large new shopping centre at its core. Telford new town includes the enormous open-air museums of Coalbrookdale and Ironbridge, where Abraham Darby first smelted iron with coke on a commercial scale. The new town was named after the architect and civil engineer, Thomas Telford who was born in Scotland in 1757 and built roads, bridges, canals and churches. He changed the face of England, for example, his canal system, 'New Cut' was a complicated web of waterways that linked all parts of the Black Country together and made the rest of England accessible.

Although ghosts are traditionally associated with the past, there are more apparitions in new houses than in old. The following is an example of a disturbance in a fairly new property in Telford:

This house is my husband's family home, he has lived in it ever since it was built in 1954. I moved in with him when we got married and my mother-in-law moved into a smaller house nearby. My mother-in-law died eight years ago. She was a very strong woman, the centre of the household.

My mother-in-law had a grandfather clock in the hall. On the very day that she died the clock stopped working. Mother-in-law died in her home just before Christmas and the day that they took her away the door opened. On the day of the funeral it was open again. The door was kept slightly ajar but I began to lock it because my great grandchildren began to pay us a visit and they thought it was wonderful to poke bits of paper through the door and watch them drop into the bottom. After a while I would find the door open although I had locked it and the lock was still across. The area in the hall around this grandfather clock is always very cold. If I find the door open, I know that something is going to happen.

One of my daughters is now 21 but when she was 15 she had a mild dose of flu and was off from school. My own parents had moved in next door, and as the electricity had gone off in our house she said she was going to her nan's to get warm. After she had come back I bumped into her in the hall and she looked deathly white. I said to her, 'What's the matter with you, anybody would think you had just seen a ghost'. She said, 'I have, I have just seen grandma in the kitchen'. I made a joke of it.

My mother-in-law visits us in dreams. Often, one of my daughters says that she dreamed about her nan in the night and she repeats a conversation.

My husband has had a sighting of his mum. He was sitting at the table in the kitchen, he happened to look up and she was standing looking at him. She just floated away into the other rooms.

She used 4711, she put it everywhere. Sometimes, we get this strong smell of 4711, it's always in the hall and it only usually lasts a few seconds. One of my daughters is fourteen and she came down the stairs a fortnight ago and said that there was a strong smell of peppermints in her bedroom. My mother-in-law ate a lot of peppermints. I think it frightened her a bit.

My eldest daughter is now 31, and she asked me if it would be alright if she took some of my mother-in-law's bed linen. I told her, 'Help yourself, have whatever you want'. We went round to the empty house and sorted out some sheets but we couldn't find the pillow cases. We went back to my house but my daughter refused to give up, she went back for a last look. When she returned she said, 'There was nothing on the bed when we left, was there?' I said that there wasn't. She went on, 'I've just found a pair of pillowcases on the bed with her new sponge bag'.

When I go over to my mother-in-law's empty house, the door opens in front of me all by itself. My dog barks and comes and sits by me. Normally, if somebody comes into the house the dog rushes out and barks at them.

Funny things happen in this house. The night my mother-in-law died the central heating broke down just at the time of her death. We were three days without central heating. Fourteen days later the dishwasher broke, the fridge broke and so did every bulb in the house – they just blew.

One night we were sitting in the dining room and we have a large display of artificial flowers on top of the T.V. It just flew off for no reason and went a couple of yards before the bowl smashed on the floor. Our ghost just does silly things, it doesn't bother me.

The Lost Church – Ironbridge

Ironbridge Gorge changed the history of the world for ever, for it was here, in the early 1700s, that Abraham Darby discovered the secret of smelting iron with coke instead of inefficient charcoal. This sparked off the whole of the industrial revolution. The Gorge is now a peaceful, rural place but in the years that followed Darby's discovery it was filled with smoke, fuel and blast furnaces.

The area was declared a world heritage site in 1986. The museum is not one museum but ten, spread across the gorge, each one preserving a part of its history. However, one piece of Ironbridge history has been lost - that of 'The Red Church'. Ron Miles, the local historian writes:

> If you search the fields in the valley south of Ironbridge where Jackfield ends and Broseley begins you will find a solitary tombstone, marked simply with the date and 'T Crump'. This single stone marks the cholera patch where the sad victims of the cholera epidemic of 1862 were brought to be buried, a cartload at a time.
>
> Why was this particular place chosen? Directly behind is a hill, on the top of which once stood a church. The cholera victims had to be interred well away from the good folks attending services on the hill to avoid spreading the disease, and so this piece on the edge of church ground was hurriedly consecrated and used.
>
> The church on top of the hill was dedicated to St. Mary. It was built of red brick with a square tower and was a landmark for miles around. Its official title was 'The Blythe Memorial Church' as Lady Blythe had it built in memory of her husband, but everyone referred to it as 'The Red Church'.
>
> Lady Blythe was a sweet and gentle lady who lived at nearby Bratch Hall. She was anxious to provide the villagers of Jackfield with a place of worship as, each Sunday, they crossed the river to Madeley Church, using a ferry which became dangerous when the waters of the River Severn were in flood.
>
> She died in 1759 soon after the plans for the church were drawn up. After her demise, the builders decided to change the building plans. Lady Blythe had expressly desired that the church should run from east to west so that the first rays of the dawn filled the chancel, but the builders decided that the church could be used as a Chapel of Rest to nearby Broseley Church and changed the foundations so that they ran from north to south.
>
> The following story comes from an undated document now in my possession, written by William Reece Evans of Jackfield. The document begins by telling how, morning after morning, the builders found their previous day's work 'all scattered about'. Consequently, two of the builders decided to keep watch during the night. The document states:
>
> *"It was a bright light, everything bathed in the silver light of the full moon. They had been waiting for some time, the chimes of the old Broseley church across the fields had just gone midnight when – 'Hark, what's that?' said one, edging close to the other. 'Look there, look there!' said the one to the other. As they both watched the*

building which had by now become visible from the surrounding field as the moon was rising, they saw the form – not of an urchin or a man – but of a lady. She picked up one of the bricklayer's hammers from amongst the various tools and, gliding along the wall of the building, she rapidly dislodged the whole of the work that had been laid that day. Then, putting the hammer back in its place again, the apparition vanished from the watching men's sight."

The two builders reported this to their Foreman, John Buchan, and it was arranged that the two men should watch again the next night, accompanied by their Foreman. They decided that they should also enlist the service of the local parson. The document continues:

"The fitful and flickering light of the lanterns gave a weird and eerie aspect to the scene. Just as midnight struck, the apparition again appeared. Holding a small crucifix in his right hand and the Bible in the other, the clergyman stepped forwards toward the spectre who had halted at the sight of the holy man. Waving the cross three times, the parson thus addressed the apparition:

'In the name of God and our Saviour who died to save all souls, here on earth and in paradise, and in the name of the Holy Spirit also, I command thee to reveal unto me thy trouble; I promise thee in the holy name of God that if this trouble can be set right it shall be done, and then I hope God Almighty will grant thee rest in peace.'

As soon as the holy man had spoke, the apparition answered, in a sweet pure clear voice. 'Reverend sire, I thank you and will disclose to you my trouble. I am the restless spirit of she who built this house of God and willed that it should be built one way only towards the east. This as you perceive, is not being done – until it is or a solemn promise made to me according to my wishes I shall not rest but shall tear it down.'

The parson made each of the party swear on the Bible that these wishes would be carried out; the apparition thanked them and disappeared.

They then built the church as to Lady Blythe's wishes. They dug up the present foundations, and relaid the church from east to west, so that the sun did indeed rise in the morning and fill the east window of the church and set again at night over Benthall and filled the other side of the church with sunshine."

The Red Church stood for just over 200 years and was demolished in 1962 because it was becoming unsafe. Perhaps someone in the twenty-first century, crossing the fields at midnight, will be accosted by an angry Lady Blythe, wanting to know what has happened to her church.

The Ouija Board – Craven Arms

Tony's family lived in Warley but every year they went on holiday to a cottage near to the Craven Arms, about three miles along the A49 north of Ludlow. This is a spectacular spot on the Welsh border, at the foot of the Long Mynd (a long low hill) and Wenlock Edge. Tony rang the well-known radio presenter, Danny Kelly, to tell him the following story:

There were about nine of us in total, my parents, my brothers and sisters and various girlfriends. I was about 24 at the time and my younger brother was 20. The cottage was miles away from anywhere, it must have been at least 400 years old and it had three bedrooms plus an extension. The locals told us that a witch had lived there in the 1600s and she had been hung from a tree outside, but we don't know if that was true or not.

One evening we decided to entertain ourselves by playing Ouija. We sat in the kitchen and we wrote out all the letters and numbers, with 'yes' and 'no' and arranged them in a circle. We all put one finger on the upturned glass tumbler in the middle.

The glass started whizzing round. It said that a spirit was trying to get in touch with us and it was that of the witch who had been hung outside. To prove who she was, she would give us the name on one of the stones in the hearth. It was just a surname and I'm afraid I can't remember it. By the time we had finished playing we were too tired and too scared to do anything about it so we went off to bed.

The hearth in the living room was apparently made up of old gravestones, they were all bits and pieces but you could just make out the lettering on some of them. We got a torch and inspected the stones and there it was! The surname was there!

We decided to play with the board again the next night. We put the youngsters in the living room with the telly on, set up in the kitchen and started playing. Suddenly, my younger brother jumped up and he went mad! He grabbed a milk bottle and started trying to kill everybody. It was very frightening. We had to call the police. Bear in mind there were no street lights, anything, and it was pitch black outside.

We were all downstairs, but upstairs something or somebody ran across the top of the stairs. We went running upstairs to see who it was but nobody was there.

The next morning we came down to find that something strange had happened. Round the house were a lot of little figurines and some of them were with wheelbarrows. During the night all the wheelbarrows had been turned upside down.

We asked the local farmer and in the local pub about the stones in the hearth. They said that centuries back, if someone wanted to build a house on a farmer's land, the farmer would say, 'If you can find enough gravestones to make a hearth you can build a house there'.

We went to the cottage again the next year but we didn't play with the Ouija board!

The house has now been turned into a Borstal.

Until recent times, if the crops failed, or if there was an epidemic or other bad luck, folks would look around for a scapegoat and accuse some poor innocent person of casting a spell. As late as 1920, a Halesowen landowner accused one of his tenants of bewitching his hounds. In England, witches were hung, in Scotland they were burned. Despite horrendous tales, not all that many people in the Midlands were hung for witchcraft although they could be imprisoned and their goods confiscated. The reign of terror that took place between 1644 and 1646 was chiefly in East Anglia.

It has been said that the reason that doctors are now chiefly male, is that the wise women, the herbalists, of past centuries had to shut up shop in fear of being accused of witchcraft. Without a doubt the Witchcraft Act of 1562 was supported by doctors who wanted to get rid of the competition from 'wise women'.

As a teenager, the author spent many a happy evening with a Ouija board without incident, however, some very strange stories have come our way. Gavin from Great Witley told us that, when the family were playing with a Ouija board, lights came on, doors banged and his uncle went berserk and ordered them out of the house. A retired engineer woke up in the night to see the head of a Victorian lady floating past his bed, his neighbours had been playing with a board. When Rita was first married she lived in Shirley in the West Midlands:

> I used to invite my friends round and we played with a Ouija board. We were playing one hot afternoon in the summer and there was this almighty bang in the kitchen. Such a huge bang, I thought, 'What the hell was that?' I opened the kitchen door and there was glass all over the floor. In one of the cupboards I had a green glass fruit bowl with six little bowls. The big fruit bowl had blown up, it had shattered into tiny pieces, and the six little bowls just sat there.

Ladies of the Night – Ludlow

The author's husband lived in Ludlow as a small boy and, sixty years later, he still raves about the town. The tragic Prince Arthur often stayed in Ludlow castle. He was the rightful heir to the throne but he died at Ludlow in his late teens so that his brother, Henry VIII, inherited the kingdom. Prince Arthur is buried in Worcester Cathedral and chroniclers say that the whole route from Ludlow to Worcester was lined with weeping people. Ludlow has the largest parish church in Shropshire, chiefly 1400s. Its streets are filled with the most impressive array of ancient buildings, including a Butter Cross and the famous Feathers Hotel of 1603.

From 1995 to the year 2000, Elaine Bell was running a café in Market Street called 'The Copper Kettle'. It was an old Merchant's House, going back to 1573.

> We used to hear strange knocking noises beneath the stairs. When we were working in one part of the kitchen we used to get the sensation that something was walking behind us, the hairs on the back of our necks would stand up and we would feel all goose-pimply. We had a little girl, a bright child,

who was a customer and she used to tell us that she could feel things. I asked the previous owners if they had any recollection of anything strange happening but they said that they hadn't.

One day, I was serving customers in the front of the building when a lady just touched me on the arm and said, 'Have you got a minute? Do you frighten easily?' I said, 'It depends what you are going to tell me'. She said, 'I'm clairvoyant and there is a lady following you around and she's sort of taking the mickey out of you. She said to tell you that she does it because you need to laugh. You haven't been very well. Does that mean anything to you?' Now I had had a period of illness and following that I kept feeling my hair being tugged. She said that there were also a lot of ladies running about in a state of undress, wearing all sorts of different clothes. Then she asked if I had had any other experiences. I told her that sometimes things moved around without explanation and she said, 'Oh yes, that would fit in'.

About six months or so after that someone came in who lived in the area and had done a lot of research into local history. We were laughing and chatting. He told me that in the old days, this was a pub called the Red Lion and it was an old coaching inn, in the 1700s the coach used to leave from here to go to London. It had the reputation of being a bit of a brothel. I suddenly remembered the conversation this woman had told me. It all fits.

This was not the only house in the Midlands apparently occupied by young ladies of questionable virtue. A clairvoyant was called in to a student flat near the Pepperpot in Upton-on-Severn, to sort out a problem. A young man was unable to sleep as he felt himself pinched and prodded all night by unseen hands. The Clairvoyant said that he was surrounded by the ghosts of teenage girls who had taken a fancy to him, and she was able to send them away. Intrigued, the occupiers looked into the history of the house and found that, in Victorian times, it had been a House of Correction for Girls.

12. Canals

In the 1700s, rivers had not been neatly channelled as they are today, and roads tended to be narrow, muddy and rutted, and were often impassable. It comes as no surprise to learn that, towards the end of that century, England was hit by Canal Mania. Between 1790 and 1797, 56 canals were constructed. By the 1830s, over 45,000 miles of canal, and rivers made navigable, were in use. So many Acts for canals were going through Parliament that it was difficult to find time for any other business. Canals helped the industrial revolution, making it possible to move raw materials and finished products easily and cheaply round Britain.

THE GRAND UNION CANAL

The Grand Union Canal is a number of short canals joining up to become one long waterway. It leaves the river Thames at Brentford and ends in Birmingham, a distance of 137 miles with 66 locks.

The Phantom Suicide – Hay Mills

About two-and-a-half miles out of Birmingham it passes through Hay Mills. Steve went fishing in the canal and:

> As we were walking back across the lock, we saw a figure at Hay Mills Bridge, going over the Kings Road. It jumped off the bridge into the water – no splash, nothing. I didn't say anything to my friend, Joe, but Joe said to me, 'Have you just seen a figure jump off the bridge?' and I said 'Yes, I was glad it wasn't only me who saw it'. This story is 100% true.

Yet another suicide. If any reader is aware of a suicide off the bridge we would be interested to hear about it.

Shades of Grey – Hatton Lock

As the Grand Union Canal winds its way towards Leamington, it passes through Hatton Lock. Bryan Godfrey had a story to tell:

> Believe it or not, this once happened to me. It was in the new year round about 1980 – something like that. My friend and I were taking four boats from Alvechurch to Fenny Compton for their winter moorings. I was on the boat 'Foxglove', it was a little boat, about thirty foot in length.
>
> When it was too dark to go any further, we moored at the top of Hatton flight. I went to bed but in the middle of the night I was woken up by my boat rocking from side to side. It felt like another boat coming along and I was

curious to know who was bringing a boat in at that late time of night. I got out of bed and stuck my head out of the hatch and I clearly saw a man and a woman mooring their boat on the other side. They were in older dress, I would say about 1920s-1930s style, she was wearing a long dress and an apron and he was wearing a waistcoat and hat – traditional boatmen's clothes. Then I went back to bed.

The next morning the boat had gone. It was only then that I realised something had been wrong. I remembered that what I had seen had been all shades of grey. I hadn't heard it go, and to come to think of it, there was no noise when it came in. I asked my friend on another boat if he had heard or seen anything, but he hadn't.

People say that I must have been dreaming but it definitely wasn't a dream.

THE WORCESTER TO BIRMINGHAM CANAL

Travellers on the railway line from Barnt Green to Birmingham, have a pleasant experience as the train passes through Edgbaston because it runs alongside a well-kept stretch of the Worcester to Birmingham Canal. From the carriage windows they can see colourful barges moving slowly along the river, while joggers and cyclists use the paths.

About four miles away, in the opposite direction from Birmingham, the canal shows a very different aspect. For here, the canal disappears into Wasthill tunnel. It starts near Hopwood, Bromsgrove, and comes up near the Cadbury Sixth Form College on the A441. At 2726 yards (2492 metres) it is one of the longest tunnels in England and was completed in 1797.

There are strange tales about the Hopwood end. Robin has a boat-owning friend:

She told me that her father worked the boats when they were horse-drawn. The footpath along the canal between Bittell and the Hopwood cutting wasn't very good, and sometimes the horse slipped, fell into the canal and drowned. Ever since then, people have reported hearing the noise of a horse trying to get out of the water.

To get through the tunnel, it was necessary for a 'legger' to lie on the boat on his back and 'walk' the boat through by walking along the walls. A legger would usually take not one but a whole string of boats through. There were several fatalities among them, especially as they were inclined to resort to 'Dutch courage' before they began the journey. A peculiarity of canal ghosts is that although several men lost their lives, the apparition usually seems to be female. In the case of Tardebigge Old Wharf, where a white lady has been seen at the entrance to the tunnel more than once, locals explain her presence by saying that she comes looking for her drowned husband. The ghost of Wasthill tunnel is also a white lady.

The White Lady of Wasthill

Andy has been crazy about boats for as long as he can remember and even a terrifying experience in Wasthill tunnel at the age of fifteen didn't dampen his ardour for long. He says:

It was about sixteen years ago now and I was with my uncle. We were travelling to Mid Warwick Yacht Club biannual bash, and were in convoy with a number of friends. The boat behind us was steered/borrowed by a 'lady' who, for modesty's sake, we will call 'Rev it up'!

On our way down she had been having trouble with an overheating engine on the boat. Well, having had a lot of experience with such engines (as much as was possible at the age of fifteen) I was volunteered by my uncle to steer the lady's boat. Let's just say that instead of her staying with the boat, she chose to travel with the aforementioned uncle.

All this aside, we approached the northern portal to the said tunnel. She disappeared into the cabin and we plunged into darkness. Now I know there are some vent shafts in the tunnel, and about two-thirds through, I thought I was approaching another one except this one seemed a bit different. For a start, it wasn't as bright as the others had been and it didn't seem as big. Well, it had probably greened over somewhere in the shaft, or so I thought. However, the closer I got, the uneasier I felt – it began to take shape.

At that point I had to stop and clear the filter on the engine, and so was lagging behind the rest. Any road up, the shape was misty, but definitely a person – all white, well grey, but you know what I mean. (As I am typing this out the hairs on the back of my neck are on end just remembering it). She (I could see it was a she) was dressed in a flowing dress, the type you see in old boatee photos, except this dress was prettier and grander than those. Well, I was about 100ft away and started to reach for the reverse lever when she faded into the darkness. I am not ashamed to say that by this time I was crying like a baby. I carried on at rather more revs than one should use in a tunnel and emerged from the other end, as my friends described, like a bat out of hell. I was white as a sheet and so badly shaken that I couldn't steer any more, and had to go and lie down.

Talking to my uncle, he told me he wouldn't go through the tunnel on his own and had been glad when his lady friend had agreed to accompany him through. He never thought we'd actually see anything but he felt better that way.

He told me that it was well-known among Brummagem boatmen that Wasthill had a grey lady. She had apparently been murdered and either thrown down the shaft, or thrown by the shaft, and had been seen regularly, mainly at night and nearly always by 'single handers'. I can't verify this story but mine is definitely spooky and I've only ever gone to Mid Warwick/Black Boy do's by road since then. Wasthill? No thanks, I'll stick to the granny cut.

BIBLIOGRAPHY

Ghosts Murders and Scandals, Anne Bradford, (2005 Hunt End Books)
Strange Meetings, Anne Bradford and Barrie Roberts (2002 Quercus)
The Centre of England, Victor Skipp (Eyre Metheun Ltd 1979)
The Buildings of England for various counties, Niklaus Pevsner (Penguin Books Ltd 1968)
The Victoria County History for various counties (University of London 1913)
Innumerable brochures, leaflets and pamphlets

The following books have been referred to in the text. They are now out of print but may be available from libraries and second-hand bookshops:
Haunted Holidays, Anne Bradford and David Taylor (2002 Hunt End Books)
Worcestershire Ghosts and Hauntings, Anne Bradford (2001 Hunt End Books)
Unquiet Spirits of Worcestershire, Anne Bradford (1999 Hunt End Books)
Midland Spirits and Spectres, Anne Bradford and Barrie Roberts (1998 Quercus)
Midland Ghosts and Hauntings, Barrie Roberts and Anne Bradford, (1994 Quercus)